FREE AND SUPER CHEAP CAMPING IN WASHINGTON

ONE HUNDRED FIVE STAR CAMPSITES FOR NATIONAL FOREST CAMPING, BUREAU OF LAND MANAGEMENT, FEDERAL, STATE, COUNTY, RV CAMPING, TENT CAMPING, BOONDOCKING

FREE AND SUPER CHEAP CAMPING SERIES

BOOK FIVE

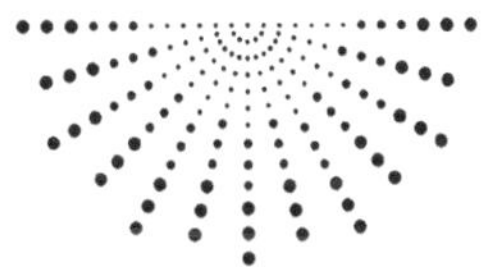

RICH SHIPLEY

WAYFARE ARTS, LLC

FREE AND SUPER CHEAP
CAMPING SERIES

FREE AND SUPER CHEAP CAMPING SERIES

The Free and Super Cheap Camping series is your passport to budget-friendly adventures across America's most beautiful public lands in:

COLORADO, UTAH, NEVADA, CALIFORNIA, OREGON, WASHINGTON, ARIZONA, NEW MEXICO

Each book features top-rated campsites, plus the tools and knowledge to help you discover thousands more. Whether you're camping in the mountains, by the sea, or in the desert, you'll find detailed information, GPS coordinates, maps, and tips to help you explore with confidence — all while keeping your travel costs low and your sense of freedom high.

SCAN OR CLICK BELOW TO SEE THE ENTIRE SERIES, AND START PLANNING YOUR NEXT CAMPING ADVENTURE.

Free and Super Cheap Camping Series: https://t2bk.com/ATT

~

Cover photo: Grand Lake, Olympic National Park, WA

Photo credit: JeffGoulden

JeffGouldenPhotography.com

iStock photo ID:1556941194

CONTENTS

INTRODUCTION

Until recently, I was living and traveling in various campers/RVs full time for almost 7 years. 95% of that time, I camped in great free or cheap places. If that sounds good, or if you want to learn about some beautiful places to camp and not spend a fortune just to be camped ridiculously close to your neighbor, follow along.

Hopefully, this book will give you some great ideas of where you might like to camp. By no means is this an exhaustive list! It's an excellent starter list, and at the end of the book, I will point you to resources with thousands of other great places to camp. More places than you could get to in a lifetime. For this book, I concentrate on some places where I and other campers have given very high ratings. I won't be including RV parks or the higher-cost campgrounds. Those are not my thing, so I can't advise you on those places, but they can be found in the resources listed at the end of the book if you're interested.

Regarding the ratings, what I, or some other people, consider a highly rated campsite may or may not be your cup of tea, or it might not be suitable for your vehicle or your camping style. Many types of camp areas are listed, from sites suitable for tents only to sites that can accommodate large RVs and motorhomes. Sites with amenities and sites with no facilities at all. A few sites might require a high clearance or a 4WD vehicle. Please read the listings, then do some research on your own to learn what you can about a potential camp area to better understand what to expect.

Each camping area listed will give you the name, whether it's free or low cost (at the time of writing), general location, GPS coordinates, the managing agency (forest service, BLM, etc.), and a brief description. **Again, once you've found something interesting, the next step in your planning would be to look the campground up by name or city/area on Google or one of the websites or apps listed at the end of this book. Please do your research! It's always best to check these to ensure you have the latest info in case of closures, fires, rough or washed-out roads, or whatever.** You'll also find more reviews on these sites and info on cell service availability, elevation, etc.

Many sites listed are first-come, first-served, while others can be reserved. Here are the common reservation websites.

www.recreation.gov For most federal lands campgrounds.

www.reserveamerica.com for state and regional parks.

Do an internet search for county park reservations.

HOW TO USE THIS BOOK

For each campground listed, you will see links and QR codes. Depending on whether you are reading the paperback, Kindle, or mobile device, you can click on a link or scan the QR code with your phone's camera. **This method allows you to see far more photos and detailed information than could ever be included in a book.**

Map: https://t2bk.com/AE

Here's a QR code example. Go ahead and try it out now.

AND FINALLY, A NOTE ABOUT THE PRICES LISTED

Most campgrounds listed are managed by the National Forest Service or Bureau of Land Management. For the campgrounds with two prices, the lower price is if you have an annual or senior pass. Information on those passes is available at the end of this book.

INTERACTIVE MAP. SCROLL AND ZOOM.

Maps: https://t2bk.com/PD

Site name numbers on the map correspond to site name numbers in the book.

Ok, enough said…

LET'S GO CAMPING IN WASHINGTON!

1

NORTHWEST/NORTH CASCADES

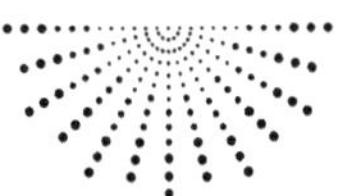

2. SOUTH BEACH CAMPGROUND - $20/$10

- Olympic National Park
- Hwy 101
- Forks, WA 98331
- GPS: 47.5663, -124.3612

Maps: https://t2bk.com/HR

SOUTH BEACH CAMPGROUND sits on a bluff overlooking the Pacific Ocean within Olympic National Park. The open, grassy campsites provide expansive coastline views with direct access to the beach below. The area is known for its dramatic ocean scenery, frequent marine wildlife sightings, and strong coastal winds. Beachcombing, tide pooling, and watching the sunset over the Pacific are popular activities. The campground is more exposed than others in the park, with little tree cover, so conditions can be windy and cool, even in summer.

There are 55 first-come, first-served campsites for tents and small RVs. Sites include a picnic table and fire ring. There are vault toilets but no potable water, electricity, or RV hookups. The campground operates seasonally, typically from late spring to early fall. Campers should bring enough water and supplies, as services are minimal and weather conditions can change quickly.

Photos: https://t2bk.com/HS

3. KALALOCH CAMPGROUND - $24/$12

- Olympic National Park
- Kalaloch Campground Rd. / Hwy 101
- Forks, WA 98331
- GPS: 47.6118, -124.3748

Maps: https://t2bk.com/HP

Kalaloch Campground is perched on a coastal bluff within Olympic National Park, offering ocean views and direct access to Kalaloch Beach. The surrounding area features driftwood-strewn shores, tide pools, and opportunities for spotting marine wildlife, including seabirds and the occasional whale offshore. The weather is often cool and misty, with strong coastal winds. Nearby, the famous Tree of Life and various hiking trails provide additional points of interest.

The campground has 170 sites for tents and RVs, some with oceanfront views. Each site includes a picnic table and fire ring. Facilities include flush toilets and potable water, but there are no RV hookups. Open year-round, the campground operates on a reservation system during peak summer months, while sites are first-come, first-served in the off-season. Due to its popularity, reservations are recommended for summer stays.

Photos: https://t2bk.com/HQ

4. BAKER LAKE ROAD DISPERSED CAMPSITE - FREE

- Mt Baker-Snoqualmie National Forest
- Baker Lake Rd.
- Concrete, WA 98237
- GPS: 48.738, -121.6084

Maps: https://t2bk.com/LJ

Baker Lake Road, or National Forest Road NF-11, offers dispersed camping within Mt. Baker-Snoqualmie National Forest. The area consists of undeveloped campsites scattered along the forested roadway. Tall evergreens and thick undergrowth offer privacy in some spots, while other sites provide easier access to the nearby lake and streams. The location is popular for hiking, fishing, and boating, with Mount Baker and North Cascades National Park within reach for further exploration.

Camping here is free and first-come, first-served, but there are no designated sites or facilities. Campers must park off the roadway without disturbing vegetation and follow Leave No Trace principles. There is no potable water, toilets, or garbage service, so visitors need to pack out all waste. Check with the local ranger district for current road conditions.

Photos: https://t2bk.com/LK

5. TINKHAM CAMPGROUND - $32/$16

- Mt. Baker-Snoqualmie National Forest
- Tinkham Rd. (NF-55)
- North Bend, WA 98045
- GPS: 47.4026, -121.5675

Map: https://t2bk.com/HT

Tinkham Campground sits in a dense forest along the South Fork Snoqualmie River within Mt. Baker-Snoqualmie National Forest. Towering evergreens provide shade and a sense of seclusion, while the river offers opportunities for fishing and wading. The surrounding area has several hiking trails, including the Twin Falls Trail and Iron Horse Trail, which wind through the forest and provide scenic views. The campground's proximity to Interstate 90 makes it an easily accessible spot for those seeking a quiet retreat in the woods.

The campground has 47 sites for tents and small RVs, each equipped with a picnic table and fire ring. Vault toilets and potable water are available, but there are no hookups. Open seasonally from late spring to early fall, sites are first-come, first-served. While the setting feels remote, the campground is close to North Bend, providing access to supplies if needed.

Photos: https://t2bk.com/HU

6. RANGER CREEK AIRSTRIP DISPERSED CAMPING - FREE

- Mt Baker-Snoqualmie National Forest
- FR-7184
- Enumclaw, WA 98022
- GPS: 47.0144, -121.5325

Maps: https://t2bk.com/HV

Ranger Creek Airstrip is in a remote, forested area of Mt. Baker-Snoqualmie National Forest, adjacent to a small backcountry airstrip. The surrounding landscape features tall evergreens, rugged mountain views, and easy access to the White River. The area is popular with hikers, off-road enthusiasts, and aviation buffs, who may spot small aircraft using the airstrip. Trails leading into the forest and up to higher elevations provide scenic overlooks of the Cascade Range.

The area is free and first-come, first-served, with no designated campsites or facilities. Bring all of your supplies and follow Leave No Trace principles. The airstrip remains active, so camping on the runway is prohibited. Access roads can be rough in places. Checking with the local ranger district for current conditions and fire restrictions is advised.

Photos: https://t2bk.com/HW

7. HOH RAINFOREST CAMPGROUND - $24/$12

- Olympic National Park
- Hoh Valley Rd.
- Forks, WA 98331
- GPS: 47.8605, -123.9348

Maps: https://t2bk.com/HX

Hoh Rainforest Campground is located within Olympic National Park near Forks, Washington. This campground has 72 sites for tents and small RVs, with picnic tables and fire rings at each site. Amenities include potable water and flush toilets, but there are no hookups or showers. The campground operates year-round on a first-come, first-served basis, with summer being the busiest season.

Situated in the heart of the Hoh Rainforest, the campground provides access to lush, temperate rainforest scenery. Nearby hiking trails, including the Hall of Mosses, Spruce Nature Trail, and the Hoh River Trail, which leads deeper into the park, are available for visitors. The area is known for its abundant mosses, ferns, and towering trees. Wildlife, such as elk and various birds, is common in the region. Campers should be prepared for wet conditions typical of the rainforest environment.

Photos: https://t2bk.com/HY

8. HEART O' THE HILLS CAMPGROUND - $24/$12

- Olympic National Park
- Hurricane Ridge Rd.
- Port Angeles, WA 98362
- GPS: 48.0361, -123.4279

Maps: https://t2bk.com/HZ

Heart O' the Hills Campground is set in a dense old-growth forest at the base of Hurricane Ridge in Olympic National Park. Towering Douglas fir, hemlock, and cedar trees create a shaded, secluded setting, with moss and ferns covering the forest floor. The area is known for its quiet atmosphere, with easy access to hiking trails and wildlife viewing. Deer and birds are commonly seen, and the nearby Hurricane Ridge Road leads to stunning mountain vistas.

Photos: https://t2bk.com/IA

The campground has 105 sites for tents and small RVs, each with a picnic table and fire ring. Flush toilets and potable water are available, but there are no hookups or showers. Open year-round, sites are first-come, first-served. The location is popular, especially in summer, so early arrival is recommended. Cool temperatures and damp conditions are common, so campers should prepare accordingly.

9. COLONIAL CREEK SOUTH CAMPGROUND - $24/$12

- North Cascades National Park
- North Cascades Hwy.
- Rockport, WA
- GPS: 48.69, -121.097

Maps: https://t2bk.com/IB

Colonial Creek South Campground sits along the shore of Diablo Lake in North Cascades National Park, surrounded by dense old-growth forest and steep mountain peaks. The lake's turquoise waters provide a striking backdrop and kayaking, fishing, and boating opportunities. Several nearby trails, including the Thunder Creek Trail, offer access to scenic hikes through the rugged terrain.

Photos: https://t2bk.com/IC

The campground has 94 sites for tents and small RVs, each with a picnic table and fire ring. Flush toilets and potable water are available, but there are no hookups. Sites are first-come, first-served outside peak season, with reservations required during summer. The campground is accessible via Highway 20, though road conditions can change with the weather. Campers should be prepared for variable mountain conditions, including cold nights and sudden rain.

10. HOZOMEEN CAMPGROUND - FREE

- North Cascades National Park
- Silver Skagit Road
- Rockport, WA 98283
- GPS: 48.9852, -121.0712

Maps: https://t2bk.com/LF

Hozomeen Campground sits at the north end of Ross Lake in North Cascades National Park, offering a remote and rugged camping experience. Surrounded by dense forest and steep mountain peaks, the area provides access to hiking, fishing, and boating. The lake's clear waters and dramatic scenery make it a scenic destination, but its isolation means campers must be fully self-sufficient. Wildlife, including black bears and deer, is common, and campers should store food properly.

The campground has 75 first-come, first-served sites for tents and small RVs, each with a picnic table and fire ring. Vault toilets are available, but there is no potable water, trash service, or hookups. Access is by boat from Ross Lake Resort or a rough gravel road from British Columbia. The road is subject to seasonal closures, so check the conditions before traveling.

Photos: https://t2bk.com/LG

11. NEWHALEM CREEK CAMPGROUND - $24/$12

- North Cascades National Park
- North Cascades Hwy.
- Marblemount, WA 98267
- GPS: 48.6706, -121.2607

Maps: https://t2bk.com/ID

Newhalem Creek Campground is surrounded by dense forest along the Skagit River in North Cascades National Park. Towering evergreens provide shade and a secluded feel, while nearby trails, such as the River Loop and Trail of the Cedars, offer easy access to scenic walks. The campground is close to the North Cascades Visitor Center and the town of Newhalem, making it a convenient base for exploring the park's rugged mountains, glaciers, and rivers.

The campground has 107 sites for tents and RVs, with picnic tables and fire rings at each site. Flush toilets and potable water are available, but there are no hookups. It is open seasonally, and sites can be reserved in advance during peak months. The location provides privacy and accessibility, though campers should prepare for damp conditions and limited cell service. Black bears are active in the area, so proper food storage is required.

Photos: https://t2bk.com/IE

12. GOAT CREEK SNO-PARK - FREE

- Okanogan-Wenatchee National Forest
- Goat Creek Rd.
- Winthrop, WA 98862
- GPS: 48.5818, -120.3738

Maps: https://t2bk.com/LH

Goat Creek Sno-Park offers dispersed camping in Okanogan-Wenatchee National Forest, providing a remote setting surrounded by dense evergreens. The area is popular in winter for snowmobiling, cross-country skiing, and snowshoeing, while summer visitors can enjoy hiking and wildlife viewing. The park sits at a higher elevation, meaning cooler temperatures year-round. There are no designated campsites, but the open forest allows for flexible camping options.

Camping here is free and first-come, first-served, with no formal facilities. Potable water, restrooms, or trash service are unavailable, so you should be fully self-sufficient and pack out all waste. The access road may require a high-clearance vehicle, especially in winter. Seasonal conditions vary, and snow can linger well into spring. Before visiting, check with the local ranger district for current road access and fire restrictions.

Photos: https://t2bk.com/LI

13. GOODELL CREEK CAMPGROUND - $20/$10

- North Cascades National Park
- North Cascades Hwy.
- Marblemount, WA 98267
- GPS: 48.672, -121.2703

Maps: https://t2bk.com/KZ

Goodell Creek Campground sits in a forested area along the Skagit River in North Cascades National Park. Surrounded by moss-covered trees and rugged mountain views, it offers a quiet, shaded setting with easy access to hiking and river activities. The nearby North Cascades Highway provides a scenic drive, and trails like the Ladder Creek Falls Trail are within a short distance. The river's cold, fast-moving waters make it unsuitable for swimming but provide excellent fishing opportunities.

The campground has 19 first-come, first-served sites for tents and small RVs, each with a picnic table and fire ring. Vault toilets are available, but there is no potable water, hookups, or trash service. Open seasonally, the campground is close to the town of Newhalem if you need basic supplies. Prepare for damp conditions, limited cell service, and potential bear activity. Proper food storage is a must.

Photos: https://t2bk.com/LA

14. MOUNTAIN LOOP SCENIC BYWAY - FREE

- Mt Baker-Snoqualmie National Forest
- Mountain Loop Highway
- Darrington, WA 98241
- GPS: 48.0712, -121.403

Maps: https://t2bk.com/LB

Camping along the Mountain Loop Scenic Byway in Mt. Baker-Snoqualmie National Forest offers a mix of developed and dispersed options in a rugged, forested landscape. The byway passes through towering evergreens, alongside rushing rivers, and near alpine lakes, providing access to hiking, fishing, and wildlife viewing. Popular trails like Gothic Basin, Lake 22, and Big Four Ice Caves are nearby, making it a prime spot for outdoor enthusiasts. Many areas experience heavy rainfall, so campers should prepare for wet conditions.

Both designated campgrounds and free dispersed camping are available along the route. Campgrounds like Verlot and Gold Basin provide basic facilities, including vault toilets and picnic tables, while dispersed sites have no amenities. Most sites are first-come, first-served, and some require a recreation pass. Check current road conditions before traveling.

Photos: https://t2bk.com/LC

15. FOGGY DEW CAMPGROUND - $10/$5

- Okanogan-Wenatchee National Forest
- NF-4300 / NF-200
- Okanogan, WA 98814
- GPS: 48.2056, -120.1963

Maps: https://t2bk.com/LD

Foggy Dew Campground is a small, forested camping area near the eastern foothills of the Cascades. Set along Foggy Dew Creek, the campground provides a quiet retreat with access to nearby trails leading into the Sawtooth Wilderness. The Foggy Dew Trail and Martin Creek Trail offer challenging hikes with scenic mountain views. Due to its lower elevation, the area is popular for horseback riding, mountain biking, and early-season backpacking.

The campground has seven first-come, first-served sites, each with a picnic table and fire ring. A vault toilet is available, but no potable water or trash service is available. The access road is gravel but suitable for most vehicles. Open seasonally, the campground can be hot and dry in the summer, with limited shade in some areas. Bring water and supplies, as services are minimal.

pgo https://t2bk.com/LE

16. SALMON LA SAC CAMPGROUND - $27/$13.50

- Okanogan-Wenatchee National Forest
- Salmon La Sac Rd.
- Ronald, WA 98940
- GPS: 47.4033, -121.0992

Maps: https://t2bk.com/LL

Salmon La Sac Campground is between the Cle Elum and Cooper Rivers, offering a peaceful, forested setting. Surrounded by tall fir trees and scenic ridges, the campground has easy access to hiking trails leading into the Alpine Lakes Wilderness. Popular routes include hikes to Waptus Lake and Polallie Ridge. The nearby rivers are ideal for fishing, swimming, and floating, while Cle Elum Lake offers additional boating opportunities.

The campground has 69 sites for tents and RVs, with some good for larger vehicles. Each site has a picnic table and fire ring. Facilities include drinking water, vault toilets, and trash collection. Reservations are available for 40 sites, with the rest on a first-come, first-served basis. Open seasonally from late May to mid-September, the campground is a popular base for summer and early fall outdoor activities.

Photos: https://t2bk.com/LM

17. TAKHLAKH LAKE CAMPGROUND - $25/$12.50

- Gifford Pinchot National Forest
- Takhkakh Loop Road
- Randle, WA 98377
- GPS: 46.2788, -121.6003

Maps: https://t2bk.com/LN

Takhlakh Lake Campground is located at 4,400 feet and offers scenic views of Mount Adams reflected in the lake's clear waters. The area is surrounded by dense forest and provides a quiet setting for camping, fishing, and hiking. The Takhlakh Loop Trail circles the lake, while the Takh Takh Meadows Trail leads to an old lava flow with expansive views. The high elevation means cooler temperatures and snow may linger into early summer.

The campground has 54 back-in sites, some designated for tents only. Each site includes a picnic table and fire ring. Vault toilets are available, but there is no potable water. Open seasonally from July to September, sites fill quickly, so early reservations are recommended. The unpaved access road can be rough, requiring slow travel. Bring sufficient water and supplies, as services in the area are limited.

Photos: https://t2bk.com/LO

18. CHUMSTICK MOUNTAIN DISPERSED CAMPING - FREE

- Okanogan-Wenatchee National Forest
- NF-7400
- Entiat, WA
- GPS: 47.6334, -120.4569

Maps: https://t2bk.com/LP

Chumstick Mountain offers remote dispersed camping with sweeping views of the surrounding ridges and valleys. The area consists of open meadows and dense forest, with rough forest roads leading to various camping spots. Hikers and off-road vehicle users frequent the area, and the summit provides panoramic vistas of the Cascade Mountains. Wildlife, including deer and black bears, is common, so proper food storage is essential.

There are no designated campsites or facilities, and camping is first-come, first-served. Potable water, toilets, or trash service are not available, so pack out all waste and bring enough supplies. Roads can be steep and rough, requiring a high-clearance vehicle. Conditions vary by season, with snow lingering into late spring. You should check road access and fire restrictions with the local ranger district before visiting.

Photos: https://t2bk.com/LQ

19. RED BRIDGE CAMPGROUND - $29/$14.50

- Mt. Baker-Snoqualmie National Forest
- 44110 Mountain Loop Hwy.
- Granite Falls, WA 98252
- GPS: 48.0709, -121.6505

Maps: https://t2bk.com/LV

Red Bridge Campground sits along the Sauk River, surrounded by dense forest and steep mountain slopes. The river provides opportunities for fishing and wading, while the surrounding area offers access to hiking trails, including the nearby Sauk Mountain Trail, which features expansive views of the North Cascades. The heavily wooded setting provides shade and a quiet atmosphere, with frequent sightings of deer, eagles, and other wildlife.

Photos: https://t2bk.com/LW

The campground has 13 first-come, first-served sites for tents and small RVs, each with a picnic table and fire ring. Vault toilets are available, but there is no potable water or hookups. Open seasonally from late spring to early fall, the campground is relatively small and can fill up quickly. The access road is gravel but navigable for most vehicles. Campers should bring their own water and prepare for cool, damp conditions, especially in early summer.

20. JOHNNY CREEK CAMPGROUND - $22/$11

- Okanogan-Wenatchee National Forest
- NF-215
- Leavenworth, WA 98826
- GPS: 47.5983, -120.8182

Maps: https://t2bk.com/JO

Johnny Creek Campground is in the Okanogan-Wenatchee National Forest, approximately 12 miles southwest of Leavenworth, Washington, at the confluence of Johnny Creek and Icicle Creek. The campground has both Upper and Lower sections, with 65 campsites suitable for tents and RVs up to 50 feet. Each campsite has a picnic table and a fire ring. Facilities also include vault toilets and potable water. There are no electrical hookups or dump stations.

The campground is open seasonally, generally from April through October, and campsites are available on a first-come, first-served basis. Visitors can enjoy various recreational activities such as hiking, fishing, and viewing wildlife. Nearby trails provide access to the Alpine Lakes Wilderness, renowned for its scenic beauty and diverse ecosystems. Icicle Creek is also a popular spot for fishing and water activities.

Photos: https://t2bk.com/JT

21. MIDDLE FORK CAMPGROUND - $32/$16

- Mt. Baker-Snoqualmie National Forest
- NF-5600
- North Bend, WA 98045
- GPS: 47.5538, -121.5375

Maps: https://t2bk.com/KA

Middle Fork Campground is located in the Mt. Baker-Snoqualmie National Forest, approximately 12 miles northeast of North Bend, Washington, along the Middle Fork of the Snoqualmie River. The campground features 39 standard sites for both tents and RVs, including two group sites equipped with picnic tables and fire rings. There are vault toilets and hand-pumped drinking water, but there are no electrical hookups or dump stations. Usually open from late May to mid-September.

The area offers excellent recreational opportunities, including hiking, fishing, and wildlife viewing. The nearby Middle Fork Trail leads to the Alpine Lakes Wilderness, known for its rugged terrain and scenic beauty. The campground is in a forested setting under a canopy of towering Douglas fir, cedar, and western hemlock trees.

Photos: https://t2bk.com/KC

22. AHTANUM CAMPGROUND - FREE

- Ahtanum State Forest
- Ahtanum Road North Fork
- Yakima, WA 98903
- GPS: 46.52, -121.013

Maps: https://t2bk.com/JW

Ahtanum Campground is in Ahtanum State Forest near Yakima, Washington, along the North Fork of Ahtanum Creek. Campsites can accommodate tents and trailers up to 32 feet, and each site has a picnic table and fire ring. There are vault toilets but no potable water or RV hookups. The campground is open seasonally, typically from late spring through early fall, with sites available on a first-come, first-served basis. A Discover Pass is required for camping.

The campground provides access to hiking, off-road vehicle riding, and snowmobiling in winter. Nearby trails, such as Grey Rock Trail and Whites Ridge Trail, lead through forested terrain with views of the Yakima Valley and Mount Adams. Wildlife, such as deer and elk, are common in the area. Campfires are allowed in designated fire rings, subject to local fire restrictions. Pack out all of your trash, as garbage collection is not provided.

Photos: https://t2bk.com/JX

23. LOST CREEK DISPERSED CAMPING - FREE

- Mt. Baker-Snoqualmie National Forest
- NF-7300
- Greenwater, WA 98022
- GPS: 47.009, -121.6181

Maps: https://t2bk.com/KR

Lost Creek Dispersed Camping is in the Mt. Baker-Snoqualmie National Forest near Greenwater, Washington. It has undeveloped sites with no facilities or water. Follow Leave No Trace principles and pack out all trash and waste. Access is via forest service roads, which can be rough and may require a high-clearance or four-wheel-drive vehicle. Camping is on a first-come, first-served basis. There is a 14-day stay limit within 30 days for all dispersed camping areas.

Photos: https://t2bk.com/KS

The surrounding area offers various recreational activities, including hiking, fishing, and wildlife viewing. Visitors can explore nearby trails through the forested landscape to experience the area's natural beauty. Huckleberry Creek runs through the area. Before planning a visit, it is advisable to check current forest regulations, fire restrictions, and road conditions.

24. HELLS CROSSING CAMPGROUND - $22/$11

- Okanogan-Wenatchee National Forest
- WA-410
- Naches, WA 98937
- GPS: 46.9647, -121.2658

Maps: https://t2bk.com/LR

Hells Crossing is a small campground in the Okanogan-Wenatchee National Forest along the American River in Washington's Cascade Range. It has 18 campsites, with 8 sites designated for tent-only camping. Each site includes a picnic table and fire ring. Facilities include vault toilets and drinking water from a hand pump. The campground is open seasonally from late May to mid-September, with sites available on a first-come, first-served basis. The narrow road has tight turns, so this campground is not suitable for large RVs.

The American River is excellent for fishing, swimming, rafting, and kayaking. The Boulder Cave National Recreation Trail offers hiking through forested terrain and a cave to explore, and nearby portions of the Pacific Crest Trail lead to scenic views. No off-road vehicle use is allowed in the campground. Firewood is available for purchase from the campground host.

Photos: https://t2bk.com/LS

25. SAUK PARK CAMPGROUND - $15

- County Park
- 54569 Concrete-Sauk Valley Rd.
- Concrete, WA 98237
- GPS: 48.4085, -121.5595

Maps: https://t2bk.com/LT

Sauk Park Campground is located along the Skagit River, surrounded by dense forest and mountain views. The area offers access to the Sauk Mountain Trail, which provides scenic hikes with views of the North Cascades. The river is popular for fishing and provides a peaceful atmosphere with frequent wildlife sightings, including deer, birds, and occasional black bears.

The campground has 28 first-come, first-served sites for tents and small RVs, each with a picnic table and fire ring. Vault toilets are available, but there is no potable water or hookups. The campground is open seasonally, typically from late spring to early fall. Campers should bring enough water and be prepared for cool, damp conditions.

Photos: https://t2bk.com/LU

26. DEER CREEK DISPERSED CAMPING - FREE

- Mt. Baker-Snoqualmie National Forest
- Deer Creek Road NF-4052
- Granite Falls, WA 98252
- GPS: 48.0851, -121.5525

Maps: https://t2bk.com/LX

Across the road from Deer Creek Campground, you will find Deer Creek Dispersed Camping. It is a remote, forested setting along Deer Creek, with dense evergreens providing shade and seclusion. The area is popular with hikers and off-road vehicle users, with trails leading deeper into the forest and up to scenic viewpoints. The creek runs alongside many campsites, creating a pleasant camping atmosphere. Wildlife, including deer and black bears, is common, so proper food storage is essential.

There are no designated campsites or facilities, and camping is first-come, first-served. Potable water, toilets, or trash service are not available, so campers must pack out all waste and bring enough supplies. The access road is unpaved and may be rough in places, requiring a high-clearance vehicle in some conditions. Snow can linger into late spring and may affect road access. Check current conditions with the local ranger district.

Photos: https://t2bk.com/LY

2

SOUTWEST WASHINGTON

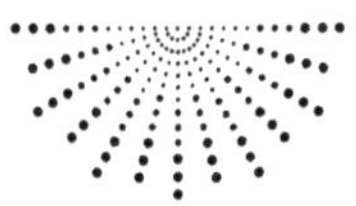

28. MOSS CREEK CAMPGROUND - $25/$12.50

- Gifford Pinchot National Forest
- Oklahoma Road
- Willard, WA 98605
- GPS: 45.7944, -121.6353

Maps: https://t2bk.com/IF

Moss Creek Campground is in the Gifford Pinchot National Forest near Carson, Washington. It has 17 campsites suitable for tents and small RVs, with picnic tables and fire rings. Basic amenities include vault toilets, but no potable water or RV hookups are available. Bring all of the water you will need. Campsites are available on a first-come, first-served basis, and the campground operates seasonally, typically from late spring to early fall.

Moss Creek Campground is forested and offers a quiet and secluded camping experience. It is located near Panther Creek and provides easy access to nearby hiking trails, such as the Falls Creek Falls Trail and the Pacific Crest Trail. The area is ideal for campers seeking a primitive, nature-focused getaway within the lush forests of southwestern Washington.

Photos: https://t2bk.com/IG

29. MIDDLE WADDELL CAMPGROUND - FREE

- Capitol State Forest
- Waddell Creek Rd. SW
- Olympia, WA 98512
- GPS: 46.939, -123.0779

Maps: https://t2bk.com/IU

Middle Waddell Campground is located in Capitol State Forest near Olympia, Washington. It has 24 campsites suitable for tents and smaller RVs, each with picnic tables and fire rings. The campground has vault toilets but no potable water or RV hookups. It is open seasonally from early spring to late fall, and campsites are available on a first-come, first-served basis. A Discover Pass is required for camping in this area.

The campground is a popular base for accessing the extensive trail network in Capitol State Forest for activities such as hiking, mountain biking, horseback riding, and off-road vehicle use. The nearby Middle Waddell Trailhead connects to multiple trails that wind through the forest. The area is in dense woods, so it's a quiet and shaded spot for outdoor recreation.

Photos: https://t2bk.com/IV

30. BEAVER CAMPGROUND - $27/$13.50

- Gifford Pinchot National Forest
- Wind River Hwy
- Carson, WA 98610
- GPS: 45.8558,-121.9596

Maps: https://t2bk.com/IH

Beaver Campground is in the Gifford Pinchot National Forest near Carson, Washington. It has 24 campsites suitable for tents and RVs, with picnic tables and fire rings at each site. The campground also has flush toilets, potable water, and a day-use picnic area. There are no RV hookups. The campground operates seasonally, typically from late spring to early fall, and campsites are available on a first-come, first-served basis.

The campground is in a forested setting near the Wind River, providing opportunities for fishing and exploring nearby trails. The Pacific Crest Trail and the Falls Creek Falls Trail are accessible within a short drive. Close to the town of Carson, it's a convenient base for exploring the forest and surrounding outdoor attractions.

Photos: https://t2bk.com/II

31. LOWER FALLS CAMPGROUND - $20/$10

- Gifford Pinchot National Forest
- NF-90
- Skamania, WA
- GPS: 46.1569, -121.88

Maps: https://t2bk.com/IJ

Lower Falls Campground is in the Gifford Pinchot National Forest near Cougar, Washington. It has 43 campsites suitable for tents and smaller RVs, each with picnic tables and fire rings. The campground has vault toilets, potable water, garbage service, and no RV hookups. It's open seasonally, typically from late spring to early fall, and sites are available on a first-come, first-served basis.

The campground is near the Lewis River, with easy access to the beautiful Lower Falls. Nearby trails, like the Lewis River Trail, offer hiking along the river and through old-growth forests. The area is ideal for fishing, photography, and nature watching.

Photos: https://t2bk.com/IK

32. PANTHER CREEK CAMPGROUND - $25/$12.50

- Gifford Pinchot National Forest
- NNF-65
- Carson, WA 98610
- GPS: 45.821, -121.876

Maps: https://t2bk.com/IL

Panther Creek Campground is in the Gifford Pinchot National Forest near Carson, Washington. It has 33 campsites for tents and smaller RVs, each with picnic tables and fire rings. The campground has vault toilets, potable water, and no RV hookups. It is open seasonally from late spring to early fall, with some sites available on a first-come, first-served basis.

The campground is in a dense forest near Panther Creek, which is near the Pacific Crest Trail. Panther Creek Falls is also close and a popular spot. Ask the campground host for recommendations for nearby hiking and waterfalls.

Photos: https://t2bk.com/IN

33. MERRILL LAKE CAMPGROUND - FREE

- Dept. Natural Resources
- NF-81
- Cougar, WA 98603
- GPS: 46.0939, -122.3198

Maps: https://t2bk.com/IO

Merrill Lake Campground is near Cougar, Washington, and has 15 primitive campsites for tents and smaller RVs. The sites include picnic tables and fire rings. The campground has vault toilets but no potable water or RV hookups. It's open seasonally, typically from spring through early fall, and all sites are available on a first-come, first-served basis.

The campground is near Merrill Lake, a fly-fishing-only lake. Non-motorized boating, kayaking, and canoeing are allowed. Old-growth forests and lava formations surround the lake, and hiking trails are nearby. The area's volcanic features and quiet environment make it a nice spot for fishing, paddling, and wildlife viewing.

Photos: https://t2bk.com/IP

34. SUNSET FALLS CAMPGROUND - $20/$10

- Gifford Pinchot National Forest
- NE Sunset Falls Rd.
- Yacolt, WA 98675
- GPS: 45.8188, -122.2523

Maps: https://t2bk.com/IS

Sunset Falls Campground is in the Gifford Pinchot National Forest near Yacolt, Washington. It has 18 campsites suitable for tents and smaller RVs, each with picnic tables and fire rings. Facilities include vault toilets and potable water, but RV hookups are not available. The Campground is open seasonally from late spring to early fall, and many sites are available on a first-come, first-served basis.

The campground is near Sunset Falls on the East Fork Lewis River, a scenic destination popular for photography and picnicking. Nearby trails provide hiking opportunities in the surrounding forest, including views of other waterfalls. Fishing and wildlife viewing are common activities along the river. The campground is a convenient base for exploring the Gifford Pinchot National Forest.

Photos: https://t2bk.com/IT

35. ROCK CREEK CAMPGROUND - FREE

- Yacolt Burn State Forest
- Northeast Dole Valley Rd.
- Yacolt, WA 98675
- GPS: 45.7639, -122.3245

Maps: https://t2bk.com/IQ

Rock Creek Campground is in Yacolt Burn State Forest near Yacolt, Washington. It has 13 campsites suitable for tents and smaller RVs, each with picnic tables and fire rings. The campground has vault toilets but no potable water or RV hookups. It is open seasonally, typically from late spring to early fall, and sites are available on a first-come, first-served basis.

The campground is near Rock Creek and surrounded by a lush forest. It is popular for fishing and wildlife viewing, and there are popular trails for hiking, mountain biking, and horseback riding. The remote setting makes it a nice option for a quiet getaway.

Photos: https://t2bk.com/IR

36. NORTH FORK CAMPGROUND - $25/$12.50

- Gifford Pinchot National Forest
- NF-23
- Randle, WA 98377
- GPS: 46.4508, -121.788

Maps: https://t2bk.com/IW

North Fork Campground is in the Gifford Pinchot National Forest, near Randle, Washington. It has 22 campsites suitable for tents and smaller RVs, each with picnic tables and fire rings. The campground has vault toilets and potable water but no RV hookups. It's open seasonally from late spring to early fall, and all sites are available on a first-come, first-served basis. Its remote location makes for a quiet spot to get away for a few days.

The campground is near the North Fork Cispus River and is surrounded by dense forest. Nearby trails like the Tongue Mountain Trail offer hiking opportunities with scenic landscape views. Fishing and wildlife viewing are popular activities in the area. It's close to the Cispus Environmental Learning Center and the surrounding wilderness, which makes it an excellent base for exploring.

Photos: https://t2bk.com/IX

37. PARADISE CREEK CAMPGROUND - $25/$12.50

- Gifford Pinchot National Forest
- Wind River Road
- Carson, WA 98610
- GPS: 45.9503, -121.938

Maps: https://t2bk.com/IY

Paradise Creek Campground is in the Gifford Pinchot National Forest near Carson, Washington. It has 42 campsites for tents and smaller RVs, each equipped with picnic tables and fire rings. The campground has vault toilets, potable water, and no RV hookups. It is open seasonally from late spring to early fall, with sites available on a first-come, first-served basis. The surrounding forest and creekside setting make it a peaceful camping spot.

The campground is near Paradise Creek, and there is easy access to several nearby trails, including the Pacific Crest Trail and shorter local routes. The area is popular for hiking, fishing, and wildlife viewing. Nearby trails offer access to old-growth forests and scenic views, making it a popular spot for outdoor recreation.

Photos: https://t2bk.com/JB

38. TRAPPER CREEK DISPERSED CAMPING - FREE

- Gifford Pinchot National Forest
- FR-5401
- Carson, WA 98610
- GPS: 45.8809, -121.9807

Maps: https://t2bk.com/JC

Trapper Creek Dispersed Camping is in the Gifford Pinchot National Forest near Carson, Washington. There are no designated campsites or developed facilities. Campers should bring their own supplies, including water, as there are no vault toilets, picnic tables, or fire rings available. Camping is on a first-come, first-served basis and is open year-round, weather permitting.

The site is near Trapper Creek, with easy access to trails such as the Trapper Creek Trail and the Dry Creek Trail. These trails offer excellent hiking opportunities through old-growth forests and along the creek. Typical activities in the area include fishing and wildlife watching, making it an excellent spot for a quiet camping experience. Please follow Leave No Trace principles and pack it in, pack it out.

Photos: https://t2bk.com/JD

39. TROUT LAKE GULER PARK - $20

- County Park
- 18 Trout Lake Park Rd.
- Trout Lake, WA 98650
- GPS: 45.997, -121.5323

Maps: https://t2bk.com/JE

Trout Lake Guler Park is in Trout Lake, Washington, in the Gifford Pinchot National Forest. The park has 15 campsites suitable for tents and smaller RVs, each equipped with picnic tables and fire rings. It offers vault toilets but does not have potable water or RV hookups. The campground is open seasonally, typically from late spring to early fall, and campsites are available on a first-come, first-served basis.

The park is near Trout Lake and is surrounded by forest, providing access to fishing, hiking, and wildlife viewing. Nearby trails, such as the Guler Ice Cave and Natural Bridges, offer unique geological features. The area is close to Mount Adams, which has more hiking and climbing opportunities. Its location provides rustic camping in a scenic, natural setting.

Photos: https://t2bk.com/JF

40. WINDY POINT CAMPGROUND - $20/$10

- Okanogan-Wenatchee National Forest
- US Hwy 12
- Naches, WA 98937
- GPS: 46.6935, -120.9079

Maps: https://t2bk.com/JG

Windy Point Campground sits along the Tieton River near Naches, Washington. It has 15 campsites for tents and smaller RVs, each equipped with picnic tables and fire rings. The campground has vault toilets and potable water but no RV hookups. Parking spurs range from 21 to 37 feet in length. It's open seasonally from May through September, with all sites first-come, first-served.

Photos: https://t2bk.com/JH

Windy Point is an excellent destination for outdoor activities. In the summer and early fall, you can enjoy hiking, fishing, hunting, horseback riding, and mountain biking. During the winter months, the area transforms into a winter wonderland, perfect for skiing, snowshoeing, and snowmobiling. Hikers and backpackers are fortunate to have access to a variety of stunning trails near the campground and in the surrounding areas. The designated Wilderness area has thousands of pristine acres to explore.

41. COUGAR ROCK CAMPGROUND - $20/$10

- Mount Rainier National Park
- Paradise Rd. E.
- Longmire, WA 98361
- GPS: 46.7674, -121.7927

Maps: https://t2bk.com/KH

Cougar Rock Campground in Mount Rainier National Park has 173 individual campsites and five group sites. Each site has a picnic table and fire grate. Facilities include flush toilets and potable water. A dump station is available near the entrance. The campground is open from late May to late September, with reservations required. The maximum RV length is 35 feet, and 27 feet for trailers. Food storage lockers are available for bear safety.

The campground is near the Nisqually River. The Wonderland Trail passes near the campground, with hiking routes to Carter Falls, Narada Falls, and other destinations. Deer and black bears are occasionally seen in the area. Park entrance fees are separate from camping fees.

Photos: https://t2bk.com/KI

3

NORTH CENTRAL

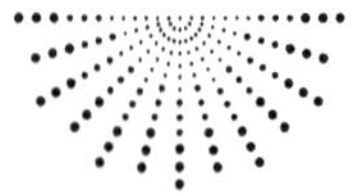

43. INDIAN CAMP CAMPGROUND - FREE

- Teanaway Community Forest
- Teanaway Rd. Middle Fork
- Cle Elum, WA 98922
- GPS: 47.2904, -120.9561

Maps: https://t2bk.com/JI

Indian Camp Campground is in the Teanaway Community Forest near Roslyn, Washington, along the Middle Fork of the Teanaway River. It has 11 regular campsites and two group sites, each with fire rings. Vault toilets are available, but there is no potable water or RV hookups. The campground is open seasonally, typically from spring through fall, with sites available on a first-come, first-served basis. A Discover Pass is required for camping.

The campground is set up for equestrian use, with horses permitted on one side of the road and non-horse sites on the other. Campfires are allowed in approved fire rings, subject to local burn bans. Garbage collection is not provided, so please pack out all trash. The surrounding area offers access to hiking and horseback riding trails to explore the scenic Teanaway Community Forest.

Photos: https://t2bk.com/JJ

44. NASON CREEK CAMPGROUND - $27/$13.50

- Okanogan-Wenatchee National Forest
- Cedar Brae Road
- Leavenworth, WA 98826
- GPS: 47.8003, -120.7135

Maps: https://t2bk.com/JM

Nason Creek Campground is approximately 19 miles north of Leavenworth, Washington, and about one mile south of Lake Wenatchee State Park. It has 70 single sites and 3 double sites, each with picnic tables, fire rings, and grills. Restrooms have electrical outlets and flush toilets, and potable water is available. There are no RV hookups. The campground is open seasonally, with 60% of the sites available for reservation and 40% on a first-come, first-served basis.

The area offers hiking, fishing, swimming, horseback riding, and mountain biking opportunities during the summer and early fall. Visitors can enjoy skiing, snowshoeing, and snowmobiling in the winter months. Attractions include the North Cascades, Lake Wenatchee State Park, and the Stevens Pass Historic District. Nearby Lake Wenatchee has excellent fishing for rainbow trout and cutthroat trout.

Photos: https://t2bk.com/JN

45. TWENTYNINE PINES CAMPGROUND - FREE

- Teanaway Community Forest
- Teanaway Rd North Fork
- Cle Elum, WA 98922
- GPS: 47.3288, -120.8538

Maps: https://t2bk.com/JK

Twentynine Pines Campground is in the Teanaway Community Forest along the North Fork Teanaway River near Cle Elum, Washington. It has 59 campsites, each with picnic tables and fire rings. Vault toilets are available, but potable water and RV hookups are not. The campground is open year-round, although not maintained or plowed in the winter. Campsites are available on a first-come, first-served basis, and a Discover Pass is required for camping.

The campground is near hiking and biking trails in the surrounding forest and river areas. Campfires are permitted in designated fire rings unless local burn bans are in place. The nearby trails are great for horseback riding and wildlife viewing. There is no garbage collection, so visitors must pack out all trash. The campground's layout allows space for both individual and group camping.

Photos: https://t2bk.com/JL

46. SNOWBERRY BOWL CAMPGROUND - $15/$7.50

- Okanogan-Wenatchee National Forest
- NF-8410
- Chelan, WA 98816
- GPS: 47.9591, -120.2898

Maps: https://t2bk.com/JR

Snowberry Bowl Campground has seven individual tent sites and two small group or RV sites that can accommodate trailers up to 25 feet. All sites include fire rings and picnic tables and are available on a first-come, first-served basis. The campground has vault toilets and a potable water spigot but no RV hookups. A group shelter with picnic tables is accessible via barrier-free trails and is available for shared use. The campground is open seasonally, typically from mid-May through October.

The campground is in the 25-Mile Creek drainage, in a quiet forest setting away from the busier regions near Lake Chelan. Popular activities include hiking on trails such as Pot Peak, Lone Peak, and Stormy Mountain. Nearby Lake Chelan is suitable for boating, fishing, and swimming. The area's varied landscapes and natural features are excellent for wildlife viewing and photography.

Photos: https://t2bk.com/JS

47. FORTUNE CREEK DISPERSED - FREE

- Okanogan-Wenatchee National Forest
- Cle Elum Valley Rd
- Ronald, WA 98940
- GPS: 47.4779, -121.0452

Maps: https://t2bk.com/JU

Fortune Creek area is in the Okanogan-Wenatchee National Forest near Ronald, Washington. There are no designated campsites or developed facilities, so campers must bring their own supplies, including water. There are no vault toilets, picnic tables, or fire rings. Camping is on a first-come, first-served basis and is open year-round, weather permitting. Follow Leave No Trace principles: Pack it in, pack it out.

The area has easy access to the Fortune Creek Jeep Trail (4W301), a challenging 6.2-mile out-and-back route popular among off-roaders. The trail leads to Gallagher Lake, known for its rugged terrain and requires high-clearance, four-wheel-drive vehicles. The surrounding forest provides opportunities for hiking, fishing, and wildlife viewing. Due to the primitive nature of the area, be prepared for backcountry conditions and check current road and weather conditions before visiting.

Photos: https://t2bk.com/JV

48. GLACIER VIEW CAMPGROUND - $22/$11

- Okanogan-Wenatchee National Forest
- NF-6750
- Leavenworth, WA 98826
- GPS: 47.8238, -120.8096

Maps: https://t2bk.com/JY

Glacier View Campground is in the Okanogan-Wenatchee National Forest on the south shore of Lake Wenatchee, about 20 miles northwest of Leavenworth, Washington. It has 23 standard non-electric sites, including 16 walk-in sites along the lakeshore. Each site has a picnic table and a fire ring. The campground has vault toilets and potable water, but there are no electrical hookups or dump stations.

The campground is open seasonally, typically from mid-May through October, and sites are available on a first-come, first-served basis. Trailers are limited to a maximum length of 15 feet. A day-use boat launch for small boats allows access to the lake for kayaking, canoeing, and fishing. A short, gentle, family-friendly hiking trail from the campground leads to Hidden Lake. The area is excellent for wildlife viewing and photography.

Photos: https://t2bk.com/JZ

49. BURKE LAKE SOUTH - FREE

- Dept. Fish & Wildlife
- White Trail Rd.
- Quincy, WA 98848
- GPS: 47.134, -119.9255

Maps: https://t2bk.com/KD

Burke Lake South is a dispersed camping area near North Bend, Washington, managed by the Washington Department of Fish and Wildlife. Camping is free and available on a first-come, first-served basis. There are no restrooms, potable water, or designated campsites. Campers need to be self-sufficient and follow Leave No Trace principles. The area is suitable for tents and small campers, with some spots offering nice lake views.

Photos: https://t2bk.com/KE

The lake provides fishing opportunities, with trout commonly stocked. Several nearby trails offer access to hiking and wildlife observation. The terrain includes forested areas and open spaces near the water. Access roads may be rough, so high-clearance vehicles are recommended. Visitors should check fire restrictions before arrival. The remote setting allows for quiet camping with excellent recreation opportunities.

50. BIG PINES CAMPGROUND - $15/$7.50

- BLM
- Canyon Rd.
- Ellensburg, WA 98926
- GPS: 46.7933, -120.4558

Maps: https://t2bk.com/KF

Big Pines Campground is in the Yakima River Canyon near Ellensburg. It has 61 sites, including two group sites and several walk-in-only sites. Each site has a picnic table and fire ring. Vault toilets are available, but there are no hookups or potable water. The campground is open year-round, with reservations accepted in high season. Otherwise, it's first-come, first-served. Discover Passes are not valid on BLM-managed lands.

Photos: https://t2bk.com/KG

The campground is next to the Yakima River, so there's good access for non-motorized boating activities such as rafting and fishing. The river is known as a Blue Ribbon trout stream, so it's catch-and-release only. The surrounding area is home to diverse wildlife, including bighorn sheep, mule deer, and over 200 species of birds, making it ideal for wildlife viewing and photography. Undeveloped hiking trails start at the northern edge of the site.

51. UMTANUM CAMPGROUND - $15/$7.50

- BLM
- WA-821 (Canyon Rd.)
- Ellensburg, WA 98926
- GPS: 46.8546, -120.4796

Maps: https://t2bk.com/KN

Umtanum Campground, located near Ellensburg, WA, along the Yakima River Canyon, provides a primitive camping experience with several sites available for $15 per night. The campground has picnic tables, fire rings, and vault toilets, but no potable water, so you'll need to bring all you'll need. It's in a popular recreational area known for its fishing opportunities in a Blue Ribbon trout stream and access to nearby hiking trails. The campground also has a footbridge for crossing the river without a boat.

The Yakima River Canyon is notable for its stunning basalt cliffs and rolling desert hills, making it ideal for viewing wildlife, including bighorn sheep and various bird species. During the summer months, the river offers family-friendly floating on the river. Umtanum Campground operates on a first-come, first-served basis in the off-season. It can get busy, so reservations are suggested during peak times, especially on weekends and holidays.

Photos: https://t2bk.com/KO

52. LOWER CHIWAWA RIVER ROAD DISPERSED CAMPSITES - FREE

- Okanogan-Wenatchee National Forest
- Lower Chiwawa River Road
- Leavenworth, WA 98826
- GPS: 47.8479, -120.6576

Maps: https://t2bk.com/KP

Lower Chiwawa River Road in the Okanogan-Wenatchee National Forest offers free dispersed camping in two large, big-rig-friendly campsites. These sites are easily accessible and provide a secluded outdoor experience. Plenty of space is available for various camping setups, including fifth wheels and travel trailers.

Photos: https://t2bk.com/KQ

The area has typical dispersed camping conditions, with no amenities like restrooms, water, or garbage dumpsters. You'll need to bring water and pack out all trash and waste. The stay limit for dispersed camping in National Forest areas is 14 days. Campfire restrictions may be in place during high fire danger, so visitors should check current fire regulations before their trip.

53. BEVERLY DUNES OHV AREA - FREE

- Dept. Natural Resources
- Road 17 SW
- Mattawa, WA 99349
- GPS: 46.83, -119.8964

Maps: https://t2bk.com/KX

Beverly Dunes Off-Highway Vehicle (OHV) Area is a 300-acre dune region near Mattawa, Washington. The terrain consists of sandy trails and small bowls, making it suitable for riders of all skill levels. The main staging area is graveled and includes an information kiosk and several pull-through spurs for camping. Facilities are limited to a vault toilet and garbage cans; there are no hookups or potable water, so come prepared.

Free camping is available on a first-come, first-served basis, and a Washington State Discover Pass is required. Campfires are prohibited. The area has scenic views of the Saddle Mountains, and the Columbia River is about 2 miles away. There is a store and gas station approximately 2 miles from the site. Before visiting, check current conditions and any restrictions that may be in place.

Photos: https://t2bk.com/KY

54. MINERAL PARK CAMPGROUND - $27/$13.50

- Mt. Baker-Snoqualmie National Forest
- Cascade River Rd.
- Marblemount, WA 98267
- GPS: 48.4636, -121.1667

Maps: https://t2bk.com/LZ

Mineral Park Campground sits along the banks of the North Fork Nooksack River, surrounded by old-growth forest and rugged mountain scenery. The dense canopy of cedar, fir, and hemlock provides ample shade, while the river offers opportunities for fishing and wading. Nearby trails, including the Elbow Lake and Hannegan Pass trails, lead into the backcountry, providing access to alpine meadows and scenic overlooks. Wildlife such as deer, black bears, and eagles are commonly seen in the area.

The campground has 21 sites for tents and small RVs, each with a picnic table and fire ring. Vault toilets are available, but there is no potable water or hookups. Open seasonally from late spring to early fall, the campground's gravel access road may be rough in places.

Photos: https://t2bk.com/MA

55. GORGE LAKE CAMPGROUND - $20/$10

- North Cascades National Park
- Diablo St.
- Rockport, WA 98283
- GPS: 48.7157, -121.1516

Maps: https://t2bk.com/MB

Gorge Lake Campground sits along the shoreline of Gorge Lake, a reservoir on the Skagit River, surrounded by steep forested slopes and rocky outcroppings. The lake provides opportunities for fishing, kayaking, and canoeing, though there is no designated boat launch. The area offers access to nearby trails, including the Diablo Lake Trail and Pyramid Lake Trail, which lead to scenic viewpoints of the surrounding mountains and glacially fed waters. Wildlife such as deer, eagles, and occasional black bears can be seen in the area.

The campground has eight first-come, first-served sites for tents and small RVs, each with a picnic table and fire ring. Vault toilets are available, but there is no potable water or hookups. Open seasonally from late spring to early fall, the campground is accessible via Highway 20. The access road is gravel but manageable for most vehicles.

Photos: https://t2bk.com/MC

56. ANTILON LAKE CAMPGROUND - FREE

- Okanogan-Wenatchee National Forest
- Grade Creek Rd.
- Manson, WA 98831
- GPS: 47.9779, -120.1629

Maps: https://t2bk.com/NL

Antilon Lake Campground is in a forested area near Manson, Washington, and is a quiet setting for camping and fishing. The lake is open to fishing, with non-motorized or electric-motor boats permitted. The surrounding landscape is dense forests, offering opportunities for wildlife viewing. While there are no formal hiking trails, the area allows for informal exploration and nature walks.

This dispersed camping area is suitable for large groups and is accessible to small RVs. Amenities include vault toilets; however, there is no potable water or trash service, so plan to pack in your own water and carry out all trash. Campsites are available on a first-come, first-served basis. Access is via Grade Creek Road #8200, which leads directly into the Antilon Lake camping area. The gravel road may have rough sections; high-clearance vehicles are recommended. Check current road conditions before visiting.

Photos: https://t2bk.com/NM

4
SOUTH CENTRAL

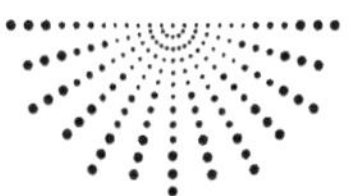

58. INDIAN CREEK CAMPGROUND - $27/$13.50

- Okanogan-Wenatchee National Forest
- NF-426
- Naches, WA
- GPS: 46.645, -121.243

Maps: https://t2bk.com/JP

Indian Creek Campground is in the Okanogan-Wenatchee National Forest along Rimrock Lake, near milepost 159.5 on Highway 12. It has 39 single sites suitable for tents and RVs up to 32 feet, each with picnic tables and fire rings. The campground has vault toilets and potable water but no electrical hookups or dump stations. The campground is open seasonally, typically from late spring through early fall, with reserved and first-come, first-served sites available.

The campground is on the edge of Rimrock Lake, which offers good fishing, boating, and swimming opportunities. The area also has access to hiking trails, including those leading into the nearby wilderness areas. Local wildlife includes mountain goats, native fish, and migratory birds. The campground's location along the White Pass Scenic Byway makes it a nice stop for travelers exploring the North Cascades Range.

Photos: https://t2bk.com/JQ

59. LOWER BAKE OVEN DISPERSED CAMPING - FREE

- Okanogan-Wenatchee National Forest
- S Fork Tieton Rd.
- Naches, WA 98937
- GPS: 46.5967, -121.2108

Maps: https://t2bk.com/KJ

Lower Bake Oven is a dispersed camping area approximately 8 miles upstream from Rimrock Lake along the South Fork of the Tieton River. This site has five large, unnumbered campsites suitable for tents and RVs, each equipped with a fire ring. There are no developed facilities, such as restrooms or potable water; therefore, campers need to be self-sufficient and follow Leave No Trace principles. Campsites are available on a first-come, first-served basis.

The surrounding area provides opportunities for fishing, hiking, and wildlife observation. The South Fork Tieton River is accessible for trout fishing. Several nearby trails offer hiking options through forested terrain, and various wildlife species can be found there. Be prepared for primitive conditions and check current forest regulations and fire restrictions.

Photos: https://t2bk.com/KK

60. JACKSON CREEK FISH CAMP - $15

- Utility Owned Recreation Facility
- 30996 Hwy 243 S.
- Mattawa, WA 99349
- GPS: 46.63, -119.8659

Maps: https://t2bk.com/KL

Jackson Creek Fish Camp, located near Mattawa, WA, is a picturesque camping destination on the Columbia River, just downstream of Priest Rapids Dam. The campground has 10 basic campsites, each with picnic tables and grills, and can accommodate trailers up to 40 feet. Facilities include ADA-compliant vault toilets. However, no water, sewer, or electrical connections are available, so visitors should bring their own drinking water.

This area is known for its wildlife and offers a range of outdoor activities, including fishing, hiking, and bird watching. The campground is open year-round on a first-come, first-served basis. Fishing enthusiasts can look forward to catching various species in the nearby Columbia River, such as chinook salmon and walleye.

Photos: https://t2bk.com/KM

61. OHANAPECOSH CAMPGROUND - $20/$10

- Mount Rainier National Park
- Ohanapecosh Rd.
- Randle, WA 98377
- GPS: 46.7365, -121.5666

Maps: https://t2bk.com/KT

Ohanapecosh Campground is in the southeast corner of Mount Rainier National Park, near the Ohanapecosh River. It has 188 individual campsites suitable for tents and RVs. Facilities include restrooms with flush toilets and drinking water. The campground is open seasonally from late May to early October. All food must be stored securely due to the presence of bears and other wildlife in the area.

The campground is in an old-growth forest at an elevation of 1,914 feet, offering an excellent environment for visitors. The Grove of the Patriarchs Trail is nearby, which leads to ancient western red cedar, Douglas fir, and western hemlock trees. Another hike is the Silver Falls Trail, which leads to views of a spectacular waterfall. Fishing in the Ohanapecosh River is permitted from early June to October 31st.

Photos: https://t2bk.com/KU

62. TREE PHONES CAMPGROUND - FREE

- Ahtanum State Forest
- A-2000 Rd.
- Yakima, WA 98903
- GPS: 46.4976, -121.1204

Maps: https://t2bk.com/MD

Tree Phones Campground is in a dense pine and fir forest within Ahtanum State Forest. It's a secluded setting popular with off-road vehicle riders, hikers, and equestrians. Several trails connect directly from the campground, with access to rugged terrain and views of the Cascade foothills. The area is home to deer, elk, and various bird species, and the thick tree cover provides ample shade.

The campground has 10 first-come, first-served sites for tents and small RVs, each with a picnic table and fire ring. Vault toilets are available, but there is no potable water or hookups. A Discover Pass is required for camping. Open seasonally from late spring to early fall, the campground is accessible via a gravel road. Check for trail conditions and fire restrictions before visiting.

Photos: https://t2bk.com/ME

63. CLOVER FLATS CAMPGROUND - FREE

- Ahtanum State Forest
- A-2000 Rd.
- Yakima, WA 98903
- GPS: 46.5071, -121.177

Maps: https://t2bk.com/MH

Clover Flats Campground is set in a high-elevation pine and fir forest within Ahtanum State Forest. It offers a remote setting with access to scenic ridges and backcountry trails. The campground is a popular base for off-road vehicle riders, hikers, and horseback riders exploring the Ahtanum area. Nearby trails lead to views of Mount Rainier and surrounding peaks, and wildlife such as elk, deer, and black bears are commonly seen. The higher elevation brings cooler temperatures, even in summer.

The campground has 10 first-come, first-served sites for tents and small RVs, each with a picnic table and fire ring. Vault toilets are available, but there is no potable water or hookups. A Discover Pass is required for camping. Open seasonally from late spring to early fall, the campground is accessed via rough forest roads that may require high clearance. Checking road conditions before visiting is recommended.

Photos: https://t2bk.com/MI

64. ROZA CAMPGROUND - $15/$7.50

- BLM
- WA-821 (Canyon Rd.)
- Yakima, WA 98901
- GPS: 46.7638, -120.455

Maps: https://t2bk.com/MJ

Roza Campground is located along the Yakima River, surrounded by rolling desert hills and steep basalt cliffs. The river is popular for fishing, particularly catch-and-release trout, and is also a well-known spot for rafting and kayaking. Wildlife like eagles, osprey, and bighorn sheep are commonly seen in the canyon. The open landscape provides little shade, and temperatures can be hot in the summer.

Photos: https://t2bk.com/MK

The campground has six sites for tents and small RVs, each with a picnic table and fire ring. Vault toilets are available, but there is no potable water or hookups. Open year-round, sites are reservable from May to mid-September and first-come, first-served the rest of the year. A boat launch provides access to the river, though motorized boats are only allowed in a half-mile section between the ramp and Roza Dam. The campground is easily accessible from Highway 821.

65. TIETON POND DISPERSED CAMPING - $8/$4

- Okanogan-Wenatchee National Forest
- NF-312
- Naches, WA 98937
- GPS: 46.6918, -121.0758

Maps: https://t2bk.com/OT

Tieton Pond Dispersed Camping is situated near Tieton Pond, surrounded by dense forest and rugged terrain. The pond and nearby South Fork Tieton River offer fishing opportunities, while trails provide access to hiking and off-road vehicle routes. Wildlife such as deer, elk, and various bird species are commonly seen. The forested setting offers plenty of shade and a sense of seclusion.

This dispersed camping area has sites suitable for tents and small RVs, each equipped with a picnic table and fire ring. Vault toilets are available, but there is no potable water or hookups. Campsites are available on a first-come, first-served basis. The campground is open seasonally, typically from late spring to early fall. Access is via Forest Service roads, which are gravel and may have rough sections; high-clearance vehicles are recommended. Check current road conditions before visiting.

Photos: https://t2bk.com/OU

66. LOST LAKE DISPERSED CAMPING AREA - FREE

- Okanogan-Wenatchee National Forest
- NF-562
- Naches, WA
- GPS: 46.6395, -121.069

Maps: https://t2bk.com/ML

Lost Lake Dispersed Camping Area sits along the shore of Lost Lake, surrounded by dense forest and rugged terrain. The lake is popular for fishing, particularly in spring, with trout being a common catch. The Lost Lake Trail provides hiking access through conifer forests with scenic views of the surrounding mountains and valleys. Wildlife such as deer, black bears, and various bird species are frequently seen in the area.

This dispersed camping area has limited space for tents and small RVs. There are no established facilities, such as potable water, restrooms, or designated fire rings. Camping is first-come, first-served. Access is via Forest Road 1200/Tieton Reservoir Road, followed by Forest Road 1201. These roads are gravel and may have rough sections. Check current road conditions before traveling, as access may be limited depending on the season.

Photos: https://t2bk.com/MM

67. PRIEST RAPIDS RECREATION AREA - FREE

- Utility Owned Recreation Facility
- 302 Desert Aire Dr N
- Mattawa, WA 99349
- GPS: 46.6841, -119.9312

Maps: https://t2bk.com/ND

Priest Rapids Recreation Area sits along the Columbia River near Mattawa, surrounded by rugged basalt cliffs and open desert terrain. The river provides boating, fishing, and wildlife viewing opportunities, with walleye, bass, and various bird species commonly found. A three-mile shoreline trail has a mix of paved and gravel sections for hiking and biking. The exposed landscape provides little shade, and strong winds are common.

The campground has 14 sites for tents and RVs, each with a picnic table, fire ring, and gravel tent pad. Vault toilets are available, and a potable water spigot is on-site, but there are no hookups. A three-lane boat launch with ADA boarding docks provides easy river access. Camping is first-come, first-served year-round, with reservations available from mid-April through September.

Photos: https://t2bk.com/NE

68. MARTHA LAKE - FREE

- Dept. Fish & Wildlife
- S Frontage Road NW
- George, WA 98824
- GPS: 47.0952, -119.8387

Maps: https://t2bk.com/NK

Martha Lake Dispersed Camping is a quiet setting near a small lake surrounded by open terrain with minimal tree cover. The lake is popular for fishing, with trout being a common catch. Birdwatchers may spot various species, especially in the early morning and evening. While there are no designated trails, the surrounding area allows for informal exploration and short nature walks. The landscape consists of sagebrush and grasses, with views of the rolling hills typical of central Washington.

This is a primitive camping area with no designated campsites. You can camp anywhere around the lake where space allows, with larger gravel areas accommodating RVs. Amenities are limited to a vault toilet, but no potable water, electricity, or trash services. Camping is first-come, first-served, with a maximum stay of three nights. A Discover Pass is required for vehicle access.

Photos: https://t2bk.com/NJ

5
NORTHEAST WASHINGTON

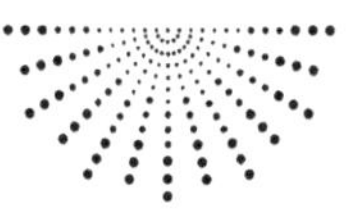

70. BONAPARTE LAKE CAMPGROUND - $20/$10

- Okanogan-Wenatchee National Forest
- Bonaparte Lake Rd.
- Tonasket, WA 98855
- GPS: 48.7956, -119.0569

Map: https://t2bk.com/PE

Bonaparte Lake Campground sits along the shore of Bonaparte Lake, surrounded by dense pine and fir forests with views of the surrounding hills. The lake is popular for fishing, with trout and kokanee among the common catches. Boating and kayaking are also possible, with a boat ramp available nearby. Several trails, including the Bonaparte Trail, lead into the mountains, offering hiking and wildlife viewing opportunities. Deer, bald eagles, and other wildlife are frequently seen around the lake.

The campground has 22 sites for tents and small RVs, some with lakefront access. Each site includes a picnic table and fire ring. Facilities include vault toilets and potable water. Some sites can be reserved in advance, while others are first-come, first-served. Open seasonally from late spring to early fall.

Photos: https://t2bk.com/PF

71. CRAWFISH LAKE CAMPGROUND - FREE

- Okanogan-Wenatchee National Forest
- NF 30-100
- Tonasket, WA 98855
- GPS: 48.4838, -119.2146

Map: https://t2bk.com/PG

Crawfish Lake Campground sits along the shore of Crawfish Lake, surrounded by a mix of pine and fir trees with open water views. The lake is popular for fishing, with rainbow trout being a common catch. Non-motorized and small motorized boats are allowed, making it a good spot for kayaking and canoeing. The area is relatively quiet, with opportunities for wildlife viewing, including deer, waterfowl, and occasional bald eagles.

The campground has 19 first-come, first-served sites for tents and small RVs, each with a picnic table and fire ring. Vault toilets are available, but there is no potable water or hookups. Open seasonally from late spring to early fall, the campground is accessible by a gravel road that may be rough in places. Checking road conditions before traveling is recommended, as access can be limited during wet weather.

Photos: https://t2bk.com/PH

72. WILLOW LANDING - FREE

- Army Corps Of Engineers
- Hastings Hill Rd.
- Pomeroy, WA 99347
- GPS: 46.682, -117.7492

Maps: https://t2bk.com/MN

Willow Landing sits along the Snake River's Lake Bryan, surrounded by rolling hills and open terrain. The river is excellent for fishing and boating, with a one-lane boat launch and a dock available. The quiet and secluded area makes it a good spot for wildlife viewing. Deer and various bird species are commonly seen. The open landscape offers little shade, and temperatures can be hot in the summer.

This primitive camping area is first-come, first-served and accommodates tents and RVs. Each site has a picnic table and fire pit, with a vault toilet available. There is no potable water or hookups. The site is open year-round, but wood fires are prohibited from June 10 to October 10; charcoal and propane fires are allowed. Access is via Deadman Road and Hasting Hill Road, with gravel sections that may be rough at times.

Photos: https://t2bk.com/MO

73. EVANS CAMPGROUND - $30/$15

- Lake Roosevelt National Recreation Area
- WA-25
- Evans, WA 99126
- GPS: 48.6978, -118.0174

Maps: https://t2bk.com/MP

Evans Campground sits along the northeastern shore of Lake Roosevelt, surrounded by ponderosa pine, Douglas fir, and maple trees. The lake is excellent for boating, fishing, swimming, and water skiing, with a year-round boat launch. Wildlife such as moose, elk, deer, and bald eagles are frequently seen in the area. The forested setting has plenty of shade and beautiful views of the lake.

The campground has 44 reservable sites for tents and RVs, each with a picnic table and fire ring. Flush toilets and drinking water are available seasonally from May through September. There are no hookups for electricity, water, or sewer. Open year-round, the campground is accessible via Highway 25, about 11 miles north of Kettle Falls. Note that water levels in the lake can vary, potentially affecting shoreline access and boat launching.

Photos: https://t2bk.com/MQ

74. HAAG COVE CAMPGROUND - $23/$11.50

- Lake Roosevelt National Recreation Area
- Haag Rd.
- Kettle Falls, WA 99141
- GPS: 48.5609, -118.1522

Maps: https://t2bk.com/MR

Haag Cove Campground sits along the western shore of Lake Roosevelt in an open space with scattered pine trees and clear views of the water. The shoreline allows easy access for fishing, and the lake is home to species such as walleye, bass, and trout. The surrounding area attracts deer and various bird species, making it a good spot for wildlife viewing. The open layout allows for expansive lake views but offers little privacy between sites.

The campground has 17 reservable sites for tents and RVs, each with a picnic table and fire ring. Vault toilets are available, but there is no potable water or hookups. All sites require reservations. There is no boat launch or dock at this location, with the nearest launch at French Rock, about 5.5 miles south. Access is via Haag Road off Inchelium Highway, approximately 83 miles north of Spokane.

Photos: https://t2bk.com/MS

75. EDGEWATER CAMPGROUND - $29/$14.50

- Colville National Forest
- Box Canyon Rd.
- Ione, WA 99139
- GPS: 48.7558, -117.4083

Maps: https://t2bk.com/MV

Edgewater Campground sits on a bluff along the east bank of the Pend Oreille River, surrounded by cedar, hemlock, and Douglas fir trees. The river provides opportunities for boating and fishing, with trout and bass being common catches. A boat ramp allows easy water access. Nearby hiking trails, including Terry Trail and Box Canyon, offer routes through forested terrain with views of the Selkirk Mountains. Moose, white-tailed deer, and various bird species are frequently seen.

The campground has 21 reservable sites for tents and RVs, each with a picnic table and fire ring. Vault toilets and drinking water are available, but there are no hookups or dump stations. Open seasonally from late spring to early fall, the campground is accessible via Box Canyon Road, about two miles north of the Ione Bridge on Highway 31. Campfires are permitted in designated rings, and pets must be leashed.

Photos: https://t2bk.com/MW

76. LITTLE TWIN LAKES CAMPGROUND - FREE

- Colville National Forest
- NF-150
- Colville, WA 99114
- GPS: 48.5745, -117.646

Maps: https://t2bk.com/MX

Little Twin Lakes Campground sits in a forested area at about 3,700 feet, offering a quiet setting next to the 49-acre Little Twin Lakes. The lakes are popular for fishing, with cutthroat trout stocked annually. Kayaking and canoeing are common, and a boat launch with a dock provides easy water access. The surrounding pine and fir forest provides shade, and moose, bald eagles, herons, turtles, and osprey are frequently seen.

The campground has seven first-come, first-served sites, each with a picnic table, fire pit, and tent pad. Vault toilets are available, but there is no drinking water or trash service. Open seasonally from late April through October, the campground is accessible via Black Lake Road and Little Twin Lakes Road. The final stretch is gravel and may be rough in places, so check road conditions before traveling.

Photos: https://t2bk.com/MY

77. WAWAWAI COUNTY PARK - $25

- County Park
- Wawawai Grade Rd.
- Colton, WA 99113
- GPS: 46.6359, -117.3728

Maps: https://t2bk.com/MZ

Wawawai County Park is in the Snake River Canyon, about three miles upstream from Lower Granite Dam. It has a half-mile interpretive hiking trail with information on the area's geology, history, and natural features. The Snake River offers fishing, boating, and wildlife viewing opportunities, with a boat ramp nearby. The landscape includes grassy areas shaded by trees, making it a good spot for picnicking and relaxing.

Photos: https://t2bk.com/NA

The campground has nine first-come, first-served sites, each with a picnic table and grill. Restrooms are available year-round, but there are no showers, electrical hookups, or a consistent potable water source. Seasonal water access is available in certain areas of the park. The park operates from 7 a.m. to dusk, with gates locked at night. A large, reservable shelter is available for group activities.

78. MILLION DOLLAR MILE NORTH DISPERSED - FREE

- Dept. Fish & Wildlife
- Coulee Blvd.
- Electric City, WA 99123
- GPS: 47.7555, -119.2244

Maps: https://t2bk.com/NB

Million Dollar Mile North is a primitive camping area near Electric City, Washington, along the shores of Banks Lake. Rugged basalt cliffs and open landscapes with lake views surround it. The lake offers boating and fishing for walleye and bass.

The camping area is primarily a large gravel parking lot adjacent to an unimproved boat launch. There are no designated campsites, picnic tables, or fire rings, and amenities are limited to vault toilets. Camping is free and available on a first-come, first-served basis, open year-round. The site can accommodate tents and RVs up to 40 feet or more. The access road is generally flat and suitable for most vehicles. Be prepared for potential wind, as the area is exposed and can experience strong gusts.

Photos: https://t2bk.com/NC

79. SPRING CANYON CAMPGROUND - $30/$15

- Lake Roosevelt National Recreation Area
- Spring Canyon Campground Rd.
- Grand Coulee, WA 99133
- GPS: 47.9333, -118.9389

Maps: https://t2bk.com/NF

Spring Canyon Campground sits on a hillside overlooking Lake Roosevelt, surrounded by a shrub-steppe landscape with sagebrush and open desert terrain. The nearby Bunchgrass Prairie Nature Trail offers a short walk through the sagebrush with opportunities to see eagles, osprey, and other wildlife. The lake, created by Grand Coulee Dam, stretches for miles and provides boating, fishing, and swimming opportunities. A day-use area includes a sandy beach, picnic areas, and a playground.

The campground has 78 reservable sites for tents and RVs, each with a picnic table and fire ring. Flush toilets and potable water are available seasonally, but there are no hookups. An RV dump station is located near the entrance. A boat ramp and docks provide lake access for water activities. Open year-round, the campground has limited services in winter when the water system is shut off.

Photos: https://t2bk.com/NG

80. BLACK PINE LAKE CAMPGROUND - $20/$10

- Okanogan-Wenatchee National Forest
- NF-43
- Twisp, WA 98856
- GPS: 48.3136, -120.273

Maps: https://t2bk.com/OD

Black Pine Lake Campground is at 4,000 feet in a forest of lodgepole pine and Douglas fir, overlooking a small alpine lake. The lake reflects the surrounding ridges and is stocked with trout, making it a popular fishing spot. Loons, osprey, and bald eagles frequent the water, while deer and black bears roam the nearby woods. A short trail loops around the lake, offering scenic views and access to quiet fishing spots. The nearby Scatter Creek Trail climbs into the Chelan-Sawtooth Wilderness, providing a more challenging hike with expansive mountain vistas.

The campground has nine sites, each with a picnic table and fire ring. Vault toilets are available, and potable water is provided in the summer. Some sites can be reserved, while others remain first-come, first-served. It's open seasonally, typically from late spring through early fall. The access road is rough in some places, so check the conditions before traveling.

Photos: https://t2bk.com/OE

81. HOOD PARK CAMPGROUND - $30/$15

- Army Corps Of Engineers
- 592 Camp Circle
- Burbank, WA 99323
- GPS: 46.215, -119.0142

Maps: https://t2bk.com/OF

Hood Park Campground sits along the banks of the Snake River, offering a mix of open grassy areas and shade from mature cottonwood trees. The river flows wide and calm here, attracting herons, eagles, and osprey. Fishing is popular, with anglers targeting bass, catfish, and salmon. A paved walking and biking trail follows the shoreline, providing access to scenic views and wildlife-watching opportunities. The nearby McNary National Wildlife Refuge offers additional birdwatching and hiking options.

The campground has 67 sites for tents and RVs, each with a picnic table and fire ring. Full hookups are available at some sites. Flush toilets, showers, and potable water are provided. Reservations are available and recommended during peak season. The campground is open from spring through fall. A boat launch and swim beach make this a popular spot for boating and water activities.

Photos: https://t2bk.com/OG

82. UPPER BOBCAT DISPERSED CAMPING - FREE

- Dept. Fish & Wildlife
- NF-51
- Winthrop, WA 98862
- GPS: 48.6309, -120.1583

Maps: https://t2bk.com/OH

Upper Bobcat Dispersed Camping sits in a rugged forested area above the Methow Valley, surrounded by a mix of ponderosa pine and Douglas fir. The terrain is rocky and uneven, with scattered meadows offering views of distant ridges. Deer, black bears, and coyotes are common, while raptors soar above the open ridgelines. Rough dirt roads and primitive trails provide access to the surrounding national forest, with opportunities for hiking, hunting, and exploring the backcountry.

This is a dispersed camping area with no designated sites or developed facilities. No restrooms, potable water, or trash services are available. Campers must pack out all waste and follow Leave No Trace principles. The area is accessible seasonally, depending on snow conditions. The rough access road may require high-clearance vehicles, and conditions can change after heavy rain or storms.

Photos: https://t2bk.com/OI

83. LOUP LOUP CAMPGROUND - $15/$7.50

- Okanogan-Wenatchee National Forest
- NF-42
- Twisp, WA 98856
- GPS: 48.3965, -119.902

Maps: https://t2bk.com/OJ

Loup Loup Campground sits in a forested setting along Highway 20, surrounded by Douglas fir, western larch, and ponderosa pine. The terrain is a mix of gently sloping hills and small meadows, with a seasonal creek running nearby. Wildlife in the area includes deer, black bears, and various songbirds. The campground provides access to nearby trails, including routes leading into the Loup Loup Summit area, which offers hiking, mountain biking, and winter recreation opportunities.

The campground has six sites, each with a picnic table and fire ring. Vault toilets are available, but there is no potable water. Sites are first-come, first-served. Open seasonally from late spring through fall. The campground is close to the highway, making it a convenient stop for travelers, but traffic noise may be noticeable. The access road is gravel but generally suitable for most vehicles.

Photos: https://t2bk.com/OK

84. LAKE LEO CAMPGROUND - $29/$14.50

- Colville National Forest
- Colville-Tiger Road
- Colville, WA 99114
- GPS: 48.6499, -117.4971

Maps: https://t2bk.com/OL

Lake Leo Campground sits at the edge of a small, forested lake surrounded by mixed conifer woods, including Douglas fir, western larch, and grand fir. The calm waters attract waterfowl like loons and mallards, while osprey and bald eagles hunt overhead. Deer are commonly seen near the shoreline, and beavers have built lodges in the shallows. A short trail loops around part of the lake, offering fishing access and views of the surrounding hills. The lake is stocked with trout, making it a popular spot for anglers.

The campground has 18 sites, each with a picnic table and fire ring. Vault toilets are available, but there is no potable water. Sites are first-come, first-served. It is open seasonally from late spring through early fall. A boat launch allows for non-motorized or electric motor boats. The gravel access road is typically passable for most vehicles.

Photos: https://t2bk.com/OM

85. DEVILS BENCH CAMPGROUND - FREE

- Army Corps Of Engineers
- Devils Canyon Rd.
- Kahlotus, WA 99335
- GPS: 46.5672, -118.5382

Maps: https://t2bk.com/ON

Devil's Bench Campground sits along the Snake River in a rugged, open landscape of rolling sagebrush and basalt cliffs. The river flows wide and slow here, attracting waterfowl, raptors, and occasional deer near the shoreline. The exposed terrain offers little shade, and strong winds are common. Nearby dirt roads provide access to the river for fishing and exploring the surrounding high desert environment.

This is a primitive campground with a few dispersed sites. There are no developed facilities, including restrooms or potable water. Campers must pack out all waste and follow Leave No Trace principles. The campground is open year-round, but road access may be difficult after heavy rain. The remote area has limited services nearby, making it best suited for self-sufficient campers.

Photos: https://t2bk.com/OO

86. LEADER LAKE CAMPGROUND - FREE

- Loup Loup State Forest
- Leader Lake Rd.
- Okanogan, WA 98840
- GPS: 48.3617, -119.6973

Maps: https://t2bk.com/OP

Leader Lake Campground sits in a dry, shrub-steppe landscape with scattered pines and rolling hills surrounding the small lake. The open terrain provides broad views, with rocky outcroppings rising along parts of the shoreline. The lake attracts waterfowl, including herons and ducks, while raptors like red-tailed hawks and ospreys hunt overhead. Fishing is popular, with the lake stocked with trout and other species. A few informal trails wind around the lake, offering access to fishing spots and viewpoints.

Photos: https://t2bk.com/OQ

The campground has several primitive campsites, each with a picnic table and fire ring. Vault toilets are available, but there is no potable water. Sites are first-come, first-served. The campground is open seasonally, typically from spring through fall. The gravel access road is suitable for most vehicles. A boat launch allows for non-motorized and electric-motor boats, making it a good spot for anglers and paddlers.

87. KETTLE RIVER CAMPGROUND - $23/$11.50

- Lake Roosevelt National Recreation Area
- Waterview Dr. / Hwy 395
- Kettle Falls, WA 99141
- GPS: 48.7164, -118.1235

Maps: https://t2bk.com/OX

Kettle River Campground sits along the banks of the Kettle River, just before it meets the Columbia River at Lake Roosevelt. The landscape is a mix of cottonwood and pine trees, providing shade along the shoreline, while open meadows extend toward the surrounding hills. The river flow is slow and calm here, attracting great blue herons, bald eagles, and osprey. Fishing is popular for bass, trout, and walleye. A short walking trail follows the river, offering water views and access to quiet fishing spots.

The campground has 13 sites for tents and small RVs, each with a picnic table and fire ring. Vault toilets and potable water are available. Some sites can be reserved, while others are first-come, first-served. It is open seasonally from spring through fall. A small boat launch provides river access for paddlers and anglers.

Maps: https://t2bk.com/OY

88. ROCKY LAKE DISPERSED CAMPING - FREE

- Dept. Natural Resources
- Rocky Lake Rd.
- Colville, WA 99114
- GPS: 48.4951, -117.871

Maps: https://t2bk.com/OV

Rocky Lake sits in a forested valley surrounded by rolling hills and a mix of pine and fir trees. The lake is relatively small, with clear water that attracts waterfowl, including mallards and Canada geese, while bald eagles and osprey hunt along the shoreline. Deer and other wildlife frequent the area, and the surrounding terrain offers opportunities for hiking and wildlife viewing. The lake is a popular fishing spot stocked with trout and best suited for small boats and kayaks.

Camping at Rocky Lake is dispersed, with no designated sites or developed facilities. There are no restrooms, potable water, or trash services. Campers must pack out all waste and follow Leave No Trace principles. The area is accessible seasonally, though road conditions may be rough or muddy after rain. The lake allows only non-motorized or electric-motor boats, keeping the setting quiet and peaceful.

Photos: https://t2bk.com/OW

6
SOUTHEAST WASHINGTON

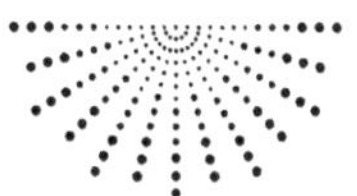

90. CAMPBELL TREE GROVE CAMPGROUND - FREE

- Olympic National Forest
- NF-2204
- Quinault, WA 98575
- GPS: 47.4823, -123.6852

Map: https://t2bk.com/PI

CAMPBELL TREE GROVE Campground is in a remote section of forest along the Humptulips River, surrounded by towering old-growth trees. The dense canopy of fir, cedar, and hemlock provides deep shade, and moss-covered trunks add to the secluded atmosphere. The river offers opportunities for fishing and wading, while nearby forest roads and trails provide access to hiking and exploring. Wildlife in the area includes deer, elk, and a variety of bird species.

The campground has 10 first-come, first-served sites for tents and small RVs, each with a picnic table and fire ring. Vault toilets are available, but there is no potable water or hookups. Open seasonally from late spring to early fall, the campground is accessed by a gravel road that may be rough in places. Checking road conditions before visiting is recommended, as heavy rain can make some sections challenging to navigate.

Photos: https://t2bk.com/PJ

91. COFFEEPOT LAKE - FREE

- BLM
- Coffee Pot Rd. E
- Harrington, WA 99134
- GPS: 47.5003, -118.5573

Maps: https://t2bk.com/PB

Coffeepot Lake camping area is in a remote high desert landscape surrounded by basalt cliffs, rolling sagebrush, and scattered grasses. The long, narrow lake is a haven for waterfowl, including pelicans, herons, and various duck species. Bald eagles and ospreys hunt along the shoreline, while mule deer and coyotes roam the surrounding terrain. The lake is known for its quality fishing, with rainbow trout and largemouth bass thriving in the deep waters.

Camping is primitive, with no designated sites or developed facilities. A vault toilet is available near the boat launch, but there is no potable water or trash service. Campers must pack out all waste and follow Leave No Trace principles. The lake is open year-round, but road access can be rough after heavy rain. The lake allows non-motorized and electric-motor boats, making it a popular spot for anglers and paddlers.

Photos: https://t2bk.com/PC

92. TUNERVILLE CAMPGROUND - FREE

- State Forest
- 5900 Rd
- Grays River, WA 98621
- GPS: 46.4208, -123.6175

Map: https://t2bk.com/PK

Tunerville Campground is a small, forested camping area near Grays River, Washington. The campground is nestled in a forest setting with a stream running through most sites, providing a serene environment for campers. The area is popular among equestrians, as it features horse corrals and access to nearby trails suitable for horseback riding.

Photos https://t2bk.com/PL

The campground has four to five sites, each with a picnic table and fire pit. Amenities include a vault toilet, but no potable water is available, so campers should bring their own supply. All sites are available on a first-come, first-served basis. A Discover Pass is required for vehicle access. Dogs are allowed on leash, and visitors are encouraged to dispose of pet waste appropriately.

93. MARGARET MCKENNY CAMPGROUND - FREE

- Capitol State Forest
- Waddell Creek Rd. SW
- Olympia, WA 98512
- GPS: 46.9271, -123.0616

Map: https://t2bk.com/PM

Margaret McKenny Campground is in a forested area within Capitol State Forest, and offers a mix of camping and equestrian facilities. Surrounded by tall evergreens, the campground provides access to a network of trails used by hikers, horseback riders, and off-road vehicle users. The nearby Fall Creek Trail System offers scenic routes through dense forest, and deer and elk are commonly seen there.

The campground has 24 first-come, first-served sites for tents and small RVs, each with a picnic table and fire ring. Vault toilets are available, but there is no potable water or hookups. A Discover Pass is required for camping. The campground is open seasonally from late spring to early fall. It includes horse corrals and staging areas for equestrian campers. Campers must register upon arrival. The camping limit is 7 days total within a 365-day period.

Photos: https://t2bk.com/PN

94. MIDDLE FORK CAMPGROUND - $32/$16

- Mt. Baker-Snoqualmie National Forest
- NF-5600
- North Bend, WA 98045
- GPS: 47.5538, -121.5375

Map: https://t2bk.com/PO

Middle Fork Campground is set along the Middle Fork Snoqualmie River, surrounded by dense forest and steep mountain slopes. The river provides opportunities for fishing and wading, while nearby trails, including the Middle Fork Trail and CCC Trail, offer hiking routes through old-growth forests with views of the surrounding peaks. Deer, black bears, and eagles are commonly seen in the area.

The campground has 39 first-come, first-served sites for tents and small RVs, each with a picnic table and fire ring. Vault toilets and potable water are available, but there are no hookups. Open seasonally from late spring to early fall, the campground is accessible via a paved but narrow and winding road. Due to its popularity, sites can fill up quickly on weekends. Campers should follow proper food storage practices, as bears are active in the area.

Photos: https://t2bk.com/PP

95. LAKE CREEK CAMPGROUND - $15/$7.50

- Okanogan-Wenatchee National Forest
- NF-51
- Entiat, WA 98822
- GPS: 47.876, -121.0143

Map: https://t2bk.com/PQ

Lake Creek Campground sits along the Entiat River, surrounded by pine forest and rugged mountain terrain. The river provides fishing and wading opportunities, and the nearby North Fork Entiat Trail offers access to scenic hikes through the surrounding wilderness. Deer, black bears, and various bird species are commonly seen in the area. The forested setting provides shade and a quiet atmosphere.

Photos: https://t2bk.com/OS

The campground has 18 sites for tents and small RVs, nine of which are available for reservation and the rest on a first-come, first-served basis. Each site includes a picnic table and fire ring. Facilities include vault toilets and potable water, but there are no hookups. Open seasonally from late spring to early fall, the campground is located along a paved road about 28 miles from Highway 97A. Check for seasonal fire restrictions and road conditions before visiting.

96. TEANAWAY CAMPGROUND - FREE

- Teanaway Community Forest
- W Fork Teanaway Rd.
- Cle Elum, WA 98922
- GPS: 447.2559, -120.8931

Map: https://t2bk.com/PR

Teanaway Campground sits in a forested valley along the West Fork Teanaway River, offering a peaceful setting with tall pine trees and open space between sites. The river provides opportunities for fishing and wading, while nearby trails lead into the surrounding hills for hiking, horseback riding, and mountain biking. Wildlife such as deer, elk, and various bird species are commonly seen in the area.

The campground has 55 first-come, first-served sites for tents and small RVs, each with a picnic table and fire ring. Multiple vault toilets are available, but there is no potable water or hookups. The gravel access road is suitable for most vehicles. Open seasonally from late spring to early fall, the campground is free to use. Check for fire restrictions and road conditions before visiting, as dry summer weather can increase fire risk.

Photos: https://t2bk.com/PS

97. FALLS CREEK CAMPGROUND - $15/$7.50

- Okanogan-Wenatchee National Forest
- NF-51
- Winthrop, WA 98862
- GPS: 48.6352, -120.1556

Map: https://t2bk.com/PT

Falls Creek Campground sits along the Chewuch River in a remote forested area, offering a quiet riverside setting. All campsites are on the riverbank, providing easy access for fishing and wading. A short, paved trail across the road leads to Falls Creek Falls, a scenic waterfall surrounded by dense pine and fir trees. The area has additional hiking opportunities, and wildlife such as deer and birds are commonly seen.

The campground has 9 first-come, first-served sites for tents and small RVs, each with a picnic table and fire ring. There are vault toilets but no potable water. Open seasonally from late spring to early fall, the campground provides a rustic camping experience. The access road is gravel but navigable for most vehicles. Check for fire restrictions and road conditions before visiting, as conditions vary throughout the season.

Photos: https://t2bk.com/PU

98. MARCUS ISLAND CAMPGROUND - $23/$11.50

- Lake Roosevelt National Recreation Area
- Orchard Lane
- Evans, WA 99126
- GPS: 48.6684, -118.0588

Maps: https://t2bk.com/NN

Marcus Island Campground is nestled within a heavily forested area along the shoreline of Lake Roosevelt, providing campers with a serene and shaded environment. During the summer months, the campground is surrounded by water on three sides, offering picturesque views and easy access to the lake. The dense canopy of trees provides ample shade and creates a habitat for various wildlife species.

Photos: https://t2bk.com/NO

The campground has 25 campsites suitable for tents and small RVs, each equipped with a picnic table and fire ring. There are vault toilets, but no water or hookups are available. All sites are available by reservation only and can be booked in advance. A small boat launch with parking is available before reaching the campground, providing access to the lake when water levels are high. The main access road is single-lane and winding, so larger vehicles should exercise caution.

99. PALOUSE EMPIRE FAIR CAMPGROUND - $25

- County Park
- 322 Fair Grounds Rd.
- Colfax, WA 99111
- GPS: 46.8669, -117.4364

Maps: https://t2bk.com/NP

Palouse Empire Fair Campground is located near Colfax, Washington, amidst the Palouse region's rolling hills and open fields. The area offers a quiet rural setting with nearby attractions such as Steptoe Butte State Park and Palouse Falls. The campground operates year-round, weather permitting, and the maximum stay is 14 days.

Photos: https://t2bk.com/NQ

The campground has approximately 147 sites suitable for both tents and RVs, each equipped with 30-amp electrical hookups, and water hookups are available seasonally, typically from mid-April to September. A self-pay station is located on-site, and reservations are not required. Camping fees and availability may differ during the annual Palouse Empire Fair in early September. Access to the campground is straightforward, with sites accommodating various vehicle sizes. Amenities include vault toilets, and a dump station is available for a fee. Pets are welcome but must be kept on a leash.

100. FOREST BOUNDARY CAMPGROUND - FREE

- Umatilla National Forest
- NF-40
- Pomeroy, WA 99347
- GPS: 46.293, -117.5585

Maps: https://t2bk.com/NR

Forest Boundary Campground is located near the edge of Umatilla National Forest, about 15 miles south of Pomeroy. It's surrounded by rolling hills and scattered pine trees, with views of Scoggin's Ridge. The campground provides access to the North/South OHV Trail, open to off-highway vehicles under 50 inches wide. Wildlife such as deer, elk, and various bird species are commonly seen in the area. The landscape is mostly open, with some shaded areas near the campsites.

The campground has six open and back-in sites, each with a picnic table and fire ring. There's a vault toilet, but no potable water or hookups are available. Camping is first-come, first-served, and open year-round, weather permitting. The main access road is paved, but some leveling may be needed for RVs within the campground. Off-road trails are easily accessible from the site.

Photos: https://t2bk.com/NS

101. HEART LAKE DISPERSED CAMPING - FREE

- Columbia Basin Wildlife Area
- Warden, WA 98857
- GPS: 46.9312, -119.1836

Maps: https://t2bk.com/NT

Scattered along the shoreline of Heart Lake, this dispersed camping area offers a rugged setting among rolling sagebrush hills and sparse stands of pine. The lake attracts waterfowl, including Canada geese and mallards, while osprey and bald eagles hunt along the shoreline. Mule deer are common in the area, and smaller mammals like coyotes and jackrabbits roam the open terrain. Nearby dirt roads and primitive trails wind through the Columbia Basin Wildlife Area, offering access to additional lakes and seasonal wetlands. The terrain is mostly open, with few shaded spots, and strong winds are common.

This is a dispersed camping area with no designated sites or developed facilities. No restrooms, potable water, or trash services are available. Campers must follow Leave No Trace principles and pack out all waste. The area is accessible year-round, though muddy conditions may limit access after heavy rain or snow.

Photos: https://t2bk.com/NU

102. TUCANNON CAMPGROUND - $8/$4

- Umatilla National Forest
- NF-160
- Pomeroy, WA 99347
- GPS: 46.243, -117.6886

Maps: https://t2bk.com/NV

Tucannon Campground sits in a narrow valley along the Tucannon River, surrounded by a mixed conifer forest with stands of ponderosa pine, Douglas fir, and grand fir. The river runs year-round, attracting deer, elk, and a variety of songbirds. Trout fishing is popular in the river, and several small, stocked lakes are a short drive away. The Tucannon River Trail follows the waterway through the valley, connecting to other routes leading to higher elevations with views of the Blue Mountains.

The campground has 17 sites for tents and small RVs, each with a picnic table and fire ring. Vault toilets are available, but there is no potable water. Sites are first-come, first-served, with no reservations. It is open from late spring through fall, with access depending on snow conditions. The gravel road to the campground can become rough, so check the conditions before traveling.

Photos: https://t2bk.com/NW

103. AYER BOAT BASIN - FREE

Army Corps Of Engineers

- Casey Rd.
- Prescott, WA 99348
- GPS: 46.5863, -118.3672

Maps: https://t2bk.com/NX

Ayer Boat Basin Campground sits along the Snake River, offering a mix of open grassland and scattered shade trees. The river flows wide and steady here, attracting bald eagles, osprey, and great blue herons. Fishing and boating are popular, with a launch providing access to the water. The surrounding terrain includes rolling hills and farmland, with a few nearby trails for walking and wildlife viewing. Sunsets over the river are often striking, with reflections shimmering on the water.

The campground has 23 sites, including options for tents and RVs. Each site has a picnic table and fire ring. Vault toilets and potable water are available. Some sites can be reserved, while others are first-come, first-served. Open year-round, though water may be shut off in colder months. The boat ramp and dock provide easy access for anglers and paddlers.

Photos: https://t2bk.com/NY

104. FISHTRAP RECREATION AREA - FREE

- BLM
- Sprague Highway Road East
- Sprague, WA 99032
- GPS: 47.334, -117.863

Maps: https://t2bk.com/NZ

Fishtrap Recreation Area sits among rolling grasslands, basalt outcroppings, and seasonal wetlands surrounding Fishtrap Lake. The landscape is a mix of open prairie and scattered pine, with rugged cliffs rising along parts of the shoreline. The lake attracts waterfowl, including pelicans, herons, and migrating ducks, while raptors such as red-tailed hawks and bald eagles hunt overhead. Mule deer and coyotes are commonly seen in the area. Several hiking trails wind through the terrain, including routes along the lake that offer views of rocky bluffs and quiet coves.

Camping is dispersed, with no designated sites or developed facilities. No restrooms, potable water, or trash services are available. Campers must pack out all waste and follow Leave No Trace principles. The lake is accessible year-round, but roads may become muddy and difficult to navigate after heavy rain or snow. The lake allows non-motorized boats and is popular for fishing.

Photos: https://t2bk.com/OA

105. KAMIAK BUTTE COUNTY PARK - $25

- County Park
- 908 Kamiak Butte Park Rd.
- Palouse, WA 99161
- GPS: 46.8691, -117.1558

Maps: https://t2bk.com/OB

Kamiak Butte County Park features a mix of dense pine forest and open meadows, rising nearly 3,600 feet above the surrounding Palouse hills. The steep slopes are covered with towering ponderosa pines, Douglas fir, and patches of wildflowers in spring and summer. The North Rim Trail climbs to the ridge, offering panoramic views of rolling farmland stretching for miles. Deer, wild turkeys, and various songbirds are common throughout the park, while the shaded forest provides a cool retreat during hot summer.

The small campground has five primitive sites, each with a picnic table and fire ring. Vault toilets are available, but there is no potable water. Sites are first-come, first-served. The park is open seasonally from spring through fall. Campers have easy access to the park's trails and picnic areas. The gravel road leading to the campground is steep in places but generally well-maintained.

Photos: https://t2bk.com/OC

106. ESCURE RANCH RECREATION AREA - FREE

- BLM
- George Knott Rd.
- Endicott, WA 99125
- GPS: 47.0143, -117.9436

Maps: https://t2bk.com/OZ

Escure Ranch Recreation Area sits in a remote stretch of rolling grasslands, basalt cliffs, and seasonal wetlands along Rock Creek. The landscape features rugged rock formations, open prairie, and scattered sagebrush, with few trees for shade. Rock Creek meanders through the valley, attracting waterfowl, raptors, and occasional mule deer. The area is popular for hiking, horseback riding, and exploring the historic remnants of the Escure Ranch. The Towell Falls Trail follows the creek, leading to a series of small waterfalls and basalt-lined pools.

Camping is primitive, with no designated sites or developed facilities. A vault toilet is available near the trailhead, but there is no potable water or trash service. Pack out all waste and follow Leave No Trace principles. Open year-round, but access roads can become muddy and difficult to navigate after heavy rain. High-clearance vehicles are recommended for rough sections of the road.

Photos: https://t2bk.com/PA

7
RESOURCES

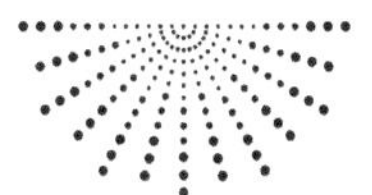

RESOURCES FOR THOUSANDS OF GREAT PLACES TO CAMP

THESE THREE ARE my go-to sites and apps to discover places to camp. I highly recommend further research on any camping area to get the latest info on seasonal closing, road or fire damage, etc.

www.campendium.com

Campendium.com is a comprehensive online resource designed for camping and RV enthusiasts to find, review, and share information about campgrounds and RV parks across the United States and Canada. You'll find detailed campground information, photos, reviews, and a convenient mobile app.

www.freecampsites.net

Freecampsites.net is an online resource that helps campers, and RVers find free and low-cost campsites across the United States and Canada. The platform offers a user-generated database of campgrounds, including reviews, GPS coordinates, and essential information to facilitate budget-friendly camping experiences.

www.ioverlander.com

iOverlander.com is a global online platform and mobile app designed for overlanders, campers, and travelers to find and share information about accommodations, camping spots, points of interest, and essential services, fostering a collaborative community for adventure-seekers worldwide.

GOVERNMENT WEBSITES FOR FURTHER RESEARCH

BLM - Bureau of Land Management www.blm.gov

U.S. Forest Service www.fs.usda.gov

Reserve America www.reserveamerica.com

Recreation.gov www.recreation.gov

Discount Passes https://store.usgs.gov/senior-annual

8
THANK YOU

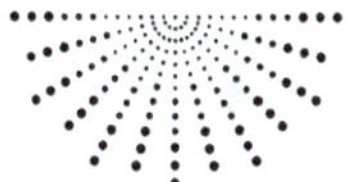

Click or Scan to hear about my next free and cheap camping book. https://amzn.to/44VJ5EG

I HOPE you have enjoyed this book and that it has given you a good idea of the vast choices you'll have in finding beautiful, secluded locations to camp on public land in Washington. Choices that won't break the bank. Choices that mean you can camp longer while spending less money. Thank you for reading. I hope you can get out there soon and have some new adventures!

To get notified when my next "free and cheap camping" book is available on Amazon, click the "Follow" button on the linked page above.

Please leave a review on Amazon!

LEAVE A REVIEW!

Enjoying this Book? Please leave a review:

Leave a review: https://t2bk.com/PW

FREE AND SUPER CHEAP CAMPING SERIES

The Free and Super Cheap Camping series is your passport to budget-friendly adventures across America's most beautiful public lands in:

COLORADO, UTAH, NEVADA, CALIFORNIA, OREGON, WASHINGTON, ARIZONA, NEW MEXICO

Each book features top-rated campsites, plus the tools and knowledge to help you discover thousands more. Whether you're camping in the mountains, by the sea, or in the desert, you'll find detailed information, GPS coordinates, maps, and tips to help you explore with confidence — all while keeping your travel costs low and your sense of freedom high.

SCAN OR CLICK BELOW TO SEE THE ENTIRE SERIES, AND START PLANNING YOUR NEXT CAMPING ADVENTURE.

Free and Super Cheap Camping Series: https://t2bk.com/ATT

www.ingramcontent.com/pod-product-compliance
Lightning Source LLC
LaVergne TN
LVHW010840120826
845149LV00017B/3333